Lifehack

Th

FULL LIFE
FRAMEWORK

· THE ESSENTIAL GUIDE ·

TO CREATE A **RICH** AND **MEANINGFUL LIFE** AND
STOP SURRENDERING TO YOUR CIRCUMSTANCES

LEON HO

FOUNDER & CEO OF LIFEHACK

The Full Life Framework,

The Essential Guide: To Create a Rich and Meaningful Life

and Stop Surrendering to Your Circumstances

Copyright © 2020 by Leon Ho

Published by LIFEHACK / STEPCASE LTD.
ISBN 978-988-74909-0-6

*To anyone and everyone who wants to live
a fulfilling life... without sacrifice.*

Table of Contents

INTRODUCTION 7

CHAPTER #1: The Reality of Sacrifice 13

The Lifehack Backstory 14

Defining a "Full Life" 21

The 6 Life Aspects...24

The Time to Live Fully is Now....................................30

Lifelong Learning is the Key to a Fulfilling Life...........32

The Full Life Assessment 35

CHAPTER #2: Your Life Is a Mission 41

Embracing Obstacles 43

...And Then My Son Was Born 48

Defining Life Missions 54

Compromise the Method, Not the Mission...............57

Connecting Life Missions to the 6 Life Aspects.......... 60

Time for Reflection...65

The Benefits of Having a Purpose............................78

CHAPTER # 3: The Progress Mindset...........................91

The Key to Lifehack's Explosion 92

Defining a Progress Mindset....................................98

The Differences Between a Progress Mindset
and a Static Mindset 100

Mindset Matters 105

Why Is Staying Inside of a Comfort Zone
Bad for Us? 108

What Keeps Us from Stepping Out of
Our Comfort Zone?...109

How to Break Out of Your Comfort Zone.......................112

True Positivity..112

Be Grateful..114

Don't Forget to Love Yourself....................................115

Keeping a Progress Mindset.......................................117

Setting Progress Based Goals....................................120

Setting Goals...122

How To Write Effective SMART Goals.........................127

Evaluating Success and Failure When Setting
SMART Goals...133

CHAPTER # 4: Self Control Systems.......................141

"The Pain in My... Back"..142

How A Self Control System Works..............................146

Creating a Good System..148

Don's Story..150

Your Self-Control System Assessment.......................154

CHAPTER # 5: The Power of Life Multipliers..............167

Life Multipliers..168

How the Multipliers Contribute to the 6 Life Aspects........178

Give Yourself a Visual Pep Talk.................................179

Recapping The Essentials..180

Strive for Work-Life Harmony....................................187

Take the Next Step..189

Recommended Reading..196

About Leon Ho..198

Introduction

A warm welcome to a book that I believe will transform your life.

This book took several months to pull together, but the background to the method behind the book goes back several years.

In 2005, I had this urge to create a personal development website. The idea for the site was the result of collecting research in an effort to help myself deal with my own struggles in life (and I had many!) and log my experiences in an organized way. I was working at a stressful job and desperately seeking a change.

After collecting a good bit of useful information from various sources and experiences, it seemed valuable to share these strategies with others, and that's how Lifehack was born. My aim for the site was to share actionable and transformational advice that would help readers reduce their stress, boost their productivity, and enhance their mental and physical health. This site would have one key objective: to help people discover how to live a better and more purposeful life.

I wish I could say that this whole process was simple... but here's the thing: life happens. And, just as you'll learn in the following pages, you often have to fail a few times before you win. But that's okay... the important thing is to always keep going.

Today Lifehack is one of the most popular personal development websites in the world. We've published over 30,000 original articles (with topics ranging from productivity tips to relationship advice), and we have millions of unique visits to our site every month. The best part of Lifehack's success is that as our audience and reach have grown over the years, so has our ability to help more people.

One great example is the wonderful Lifehack Insider Community we have. With a strong community of over 500,000 members, and a daily email newsletter written by me, it's an easy way to get a dose of daily inspiration. We also publish a regular podcast, The Lifehack Show, which features exclusive interviews with experts in life improvement from various backgrounds. And last — but definitely not least — we have a number of comprehensive online courses covering topics such as increasing motivation, accelerating learning, and sharpening focus. These self-study courses go much deeper than our articles, and the in-depth guidance as well as personalized coaching frequently leads to personal breakthroughs.

We're always searching for ways to improve our content and to help as many people as we possibly can.

That's the reason for this book!

As there are many people who are happy to dip in and learn from the articles on our website, there are others who prefer a more detailed and structured approach to learning how to fast-track themselves towards a Full Life. This is what I'm aiming to provide to you in the following pages.

So, before we get started, let me tell you about the two key things that you're going to take away from this book:

1. Self-awareness.
2. A tangible method of transforming your life into a 'Full Life'.

When you begin to put these two things into action (as I'll show you exactly how to do) — you'll quickly begin to create the life you've always dreamed of.

And this brings me to the beginning of this book, which includes my own story of doing just that, when I realized that Lifehack was more than just a hobby.

#01

CHAPTER

The Reality of Sacrifice

"If you really want to live your life to the fullest and realize your greatest potential, you must be willing to run the risk of making some people mad. People may not like what you do, people may not like how you do it, but these people are not living your life. You are!"

— *Iyanla Vanzant*

The Lifehack Backstory

It was New Year's Eve in 2006, and I was sitting alone in my corner office at Red Hat — a global software company of which I had been quickly climbing the corporate ladder. I should have been happy that the New Year celebrations were gearing up, but I was struggling to get in the mood.

The problem was, I was stuck at a crossroads.

You see, I had been very successful in the traditional sense of the word (I had a beautiful sports car, a lovely home, and an even lovelier fiance), but I had also begun to feel the twinges of unhappiness and dissatisfaction with my life. I was working too much and still not feeling like I was accomplishing enough. I knew that if I continued along this path, I might increase my income, but I'd lose my sense of self and turn into a depressed — and stressed — workaholic. I might boost my bank account, but I'd never have the chance to fulfill my dreams.

The dilemma that I was facing was this: In just under a year, Lifehack had started to gain a strong and dedicated following. As I watched the blog grow and the positive feedback from readers stream in, I'd begun to realize that this is something I was passionate about, and something I'd love to dedicate my life to. I imagined a fulfilled life being able to run Lifehack as a business.

So as I sat alone in the office, I asked myself:

Should I continue along my current career path, where I'm guaranteed success in the traditional sense — or should I take a massive risk by pursuing my dream?

My mind raced between thoughts of both scenarios, while my emotions went on a roller coaster ride with what to do. But it wasn't long before it became crystal clear that if I was ever going to break free from my self-imposed misery — then this was the time to do it!

Looking back at that night, I realize that it all happened at once. After spending hours contemplating my future, I suddenly made the decision to leave Red Hat and to pursue my dream of running my own business by turning Lifehack into a full-time venture.

And once I'd made that decision, I felt an incredible sense of relief. It was like a heavy load had been lifted off my shoulders. I was free. I was happy. And I was now ready to join the New Year celebrations!

Of course, not everyone shared my enthusiasm. You see, major career changes like this aren't usually easy or taken lightly. And this was quickly in evidence when I excitedly shared my plans with my friends and family. Some were supportive, but most weren't.

The responses I got varied:

"Why are you throwing away your career?"

"This is not a good idea, Leon. "

... and my favorite, "Are you nuts?!"

But my mind was made up. This was a mission that I needed to fulfill--and I believed I could. So, I wasn't going to let negative comments knock me off course. This is something that I wanted to make happen and I was determined to do it.

After finishing my last few weeks with Red Hat, I was ready to begin taking on the challenge of turning Lifehack into a revenue generating full-time career. It was an enormous amount of work and effort, but I quickly fell in love with being an entrepreneur. I was in my element for the very first time in my life.

Fortunately — due to my hard work, persistence and creativity — it was just a matter of months before Lifehack's audience had grown big enough to justify me hiring my first members of staff.

It wasn't long before we were gaining hundreds of new readers and followers every single day. I was thrilled by our success!

But, with the benefit of hindsight, I can now see that Lifehack's rapid success came on way too quickly.

How do I know this?

Because the success came with a heavy personal price...

For instance, I had less income since quitting Red Hat, and I was often trying desperately to catch up financially. And, due to my intense commitment to running and growing Lifehack, my new marriage began to be strained. I hadn't realized this at first (despite the many hints from my wife), but as I grew stronger as an entrepreneur, I grew more distant as a husband. And when it finally dawned on me, I felt ashamed about having spent most of my time on my business rather than spending it with my wife.

And this wasn't the only thing that was going wrong.

I also noticed that my physical and mental health was starting to deteriorate. This included developing back pain and having trouble sleeping at night. I felt like I was beginning to fall apart, and I was overwhelmed in all areas of my life.

I had countless things to do to keep my business going, countless things to do to keep my family happy, and countless things to do to try and keep myself together!

It was a challenge that I thought I could defeat by working harder and longer. But as time went on, I eventually realized that if I didn't change my approach to work and life — I would probably end up having a breakdown.

It was ironic really. Here I was creating and sharing self-development content that was helping thousands of people in tangible ways, while I was struggling to keep my own life on track.

As American author Arthur Golden poetically said:

"Adversity is like a strong wind. It tears away from us all but the things that cannot be torn, so that we see ourselves as we really are."

This quote sums up exactly what was happening to me at that time. I was outwardly succeeding, but inwardly failing. And my prosperity had turned into adversity.

So what was I to do?

I contemplated this question for many days and nights. And I kept telling myself that there must be a solution to my problems. Fortunately, there was.

It occurred to me one night that I was always trying to fix one area of my life at a time. For example, if I needed more time for my business then I would simply steal some from another area of my life.

This included regularly cancelling meetups with friends, and not prioritizing time with my wife.

Despite having read and written extensively on the topic of holistic living, I was actually living in a fragmented personal world. A world that was so compartmentalized that nothing flowed between the different areas of my life. There was no balance or harmony.

Upon realizing my self-inflicted predicament, I decided to do something about it.

I immediately went to work in creating a plan that would put my life back into equilibrium. And when the plan was finally finished, I could see that I had discovered a little-known and seldom-applied key to success and happiness. No more would I try to fix individual parts of my life. Instead, I would follow the pathway that would transform ALL areas of my life at once.

I literally reinvented my approach to life. And this set the stage for everything I would do in my life going forward.

It was also at this time that I developed a concept called 'Life Multipliers' — skills that can bring positive change to many aspects of life all at once (I'll go more into detail on these later on). With my new insight and direction, I was more empowered and confident than I had ever felt before. So much so, that I felt as though I could overcome any new obstacles that came my way. And, best of all, I had a much clearer mindset to understand where I wanted to go.

There was also a distinctive difference in my approach to life. Before, I felt trapped by my personal circumstances; but now I was living a life of choice and freedom. I could do the things I wanted to do and help the people I wanted to help.

This new mindset was a major turning point for me. And after I saw how powerful it was in my personal life, I quickly adopted it as the basis of our mission at Lifehack.

I've given you a glimpse into my background and personal experiences, as I wanted you to see that my success today has not been due to luck or having been born with a silver spoon in my mouth. It's been a long time of experimenting to find out what works — and what doesn't work.

Today, I'm the person I've always wanted to be: a person who enjoys a *full life without any sacrifice*. I recognize and appreciate the ongoing growth in my personal health, fitness, family (now with two incredible sons) and business.

I now understand that when I'm healthier, I have more energy to do my work in an impactful way and enjoy more time with my family. And I see how my physical health and family relationships affect my mental capacity as well — helping me to become a better communicator at home. And when I have better communication with my wife, I am much happier overall, and my motivation and positivity at work are heightened. And when I invest time and energy into my kids, it only strengthens that bond with my wife, which in turn, grows my business and helps me to look forward to my future even more.

Taking care of my mental and physical health, and not putting it on the back burner, has allowed me to become so much more equipped to deal with conflict.

This has been truly life-changing for me. And, this is the basis of our Full Life Framework.

Now, please don't get me wrong, the framework I've developed hasn't transformed me into any sort of superhero. I'm still just a regular person with 24 hours in each day. But my mindset and habits have shifted significantly — giving me a unique perspective on life. This has allowed me to excel in all areas of my life and really feel like I'm living fully.

The mindset and skills that I've implemented have become a core part of everything Lifehack does and offers. As you may have noticed, we're constantly moving forward and improving.

One key insight I can give you right now is this:

All limitations start from your mind. This means that if you can learn to take control of your mind and your thoughts — you can break free from your limitations.

I'll show you exactly how to do this as I go through the steps that make up our 'Full Life Framework'. This framework is an expansion and improvement on my original Life Multipliers concept.

By going through each step of this powerful framework, you'll be able to transform your mindset and actions. And ultimately, you'll be able to achieve any goal you set your mind to.

Defining a "Full Life"

Do you desire happiness?

Of course, everyone wants to be happy! The essence of what you do or where you want to go is to increase your level of personal satisfaction. However, sometimes the efforts you take to improve your happiness don't pan out.

Perhaps you are gathering material assets or working extra hours to increase your bank balance. While material assets and money are vital components of staying happy, they cannot bring lasting happiness.

Truly, lasting happiness is reached by living a Full Life.

So what does it mean to live a Full Life? Is it possible to achieve balance in every aspect of your life?

The word 'full' means the ability to enforce positive change in major aspects of your life. It is not enough to focus on one aspect to the detriment of others. You need to experience success in multiple areas to achieve a full life status.

One thing to make clear: *A Full Life does not equal a perfect life.*

While perfectionism usually exists as the obsession of wanting something to be exactly right, the desire for it actually can prevent us from living a full life. Because, let's face it, nothing is perfect — especially one's life. And, the truth is, everyone's idea of a full life is totally individual, which also skews the definition of "perfect".

Perfectionism is born out of uneasiness, concern and doubt rather than a basic want to do things well.

How you define "success" matters too. Recall my story about leaving Red Hat. According to many, I was "successful", but personally, I wasn't happy. So, my definition of success is likely very different than yours.

Living your life to the fullest means maximizing your innate potential and creating possibilities that affect every department of your life — and to make it meaningful. The person who lives life to the fullest can face their fears, open their mind, and shun mediocrity. They can maximize their time and refuse to settle for nothing less than their capability.

There exists a significant relationship among every aspect of your life.

Your health affects your wealth and vice versa. Your relationships determine your career growth. So, if you invest in each of them equally, you will reap the rewards of a tremendously full life.

You can be happy at home, and still be productive at work. You really can have it all!

Paul's Story

I'd like to share the story of Paul, one of our students. Paul is a single dad of 4 who was feeling overwhelmed with life and sought out help from Lifehack. He was working at two jobs, and didn't have the time to achieve anything outside of work, and was starting to feel the impacts of burnout.

His health was deteriorating, and he was up for retirement for one career. He had no clue what he should do to help his situation—he felt completely and totally stuck. According to Paul, " I felt like life was running me, and I wasn't running life."

So, Paul committed to making a change and started with our Full Life Framework.

Here's the strategy Paul adopted. He would stay later after work to try and complete a module once everyone had left the office. This time alone also afforded him the time to reflect on his personal life.

During this time Paul learned a major life lesson: self-care is not selfish.

Self-care is a product of love, while selfishness is a product of fear. You cannot attain a full life when fear controls your life. The resources you need to achieve a full life are within your reach.

Paul was able to discover how to make improvements in all areas of his life, including how to better understand himself and his own needs, how to adopt a Progress mindset, and how to make habits and routines work for him.

With this Full Life mindset, Paul was able to transform an overwhelming life event (his retirement) into a positive opportunity for growth towards his own idea of a happy and full life. He also learned the importance of the 6 Life Aspects, and recognized where he needed to make the most improvements.

The 6 Life Aspects

There's a theory out there called "the four-burner theory", which states that you have four major burners in your life: your family, your friends, your health, and your work. The theory affirmed that for you to be successful, you need to sacrifice at least one of the burners as you can only cope with three at a time.

But, here's the thing: this theory couldn't be further from the truth.

You can absolutely live your life without trade-offs or sacrifice, if you embrace a Full Life mindset.

Let's start by understanding the basis of a Full Life: The 6 Life Aspects.

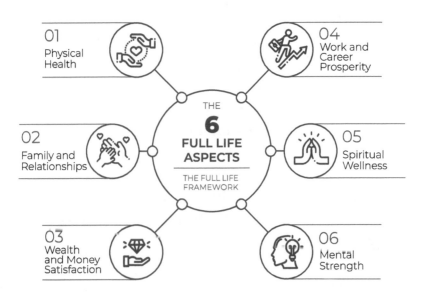

Together, the 6 Life Aspects form a complete picture of living a full life. Every aspect is essential to the other and therefore, none can fully exist if you try to sacrifice one area.

Living a full life requires you to balance among all these aspects at once:

1. Physical Health
2. Family and Relationships
3. Wealth and Money Satisfaction
4. Work and Career Prosperity
5. Spiritual Wellness
6. Mental Strength

If you focus too much on one aspect, you will likely risk sacrificing another aspect. This is the more reason you need to have a whole picture perspective to life and practice harmony. In short, each Life Aspect should get about the same level of attention and nurturing.

Below, I've broken each Life Aspect down for you to better understand the importance of each.

Allow every aspect of your life to collaborate together instead of competing with one another. Stop separating your time into work-time, personal-time, social-time, and other unnecessary compartments. Eliminate any imaginary lines to ease yourself of tension and see where they can overlap (just like Paul spending extra time after work to complete a Lifehack course).

Physical Health

Physical Health encompasses your habits that lead to your overall well being as well as how you take care of your physical body. It includes your diet, daily exercise, eating and drinking habits, hygiene, your posture, your sleeping habits, and how you conduct yourself. According to a recent study on mood and physical activity, people who exercise even once a week or for as little as 10 minutes a day tend to be more cheerful than those who never exercise. And, the best part? Any type of exercise is helpful!

It's pretty obvious that you cannot achieve success in any area of your life without your physical body. Therefore, the first step to achieve a full life and be happy is to take good care of yourself physically — to treat your body as your temple.

Make it a priority to cultivate healthy habits such as eating a well balanced diet, getting enough sleep each night, drinking at least eight glasses of water daily, and exercising regularly.

A healthy body produces a healthy mind. Staying in good physical shape will enable you to become more confident, inspired, energized, and ultimately, happy.

Family and Relationships

There's no denying it: relationships are difficult. Yet, there is a lot of science-backed research that points to the importance of cultivating healthy and happy relationships in life.

Empathy, positivity and a strong emotional connection drive

the happiest and healthiest relationships, whether romantic or among colleagues. Strong and healthy relationships are crucial to a Full Life.

Wealth and Money Satisfaction

Another way to look at this is by seeing it as a level of financial freedom. You don't need to be rich, you simply need to have enough money and sufficient time to enjoy it. The reason most people work extra hours is to make more money. Yet, oftentimes, the rich make a lot of money with no time to spend it while the poor have more time with no money to enjoy it.

Living a full life means you have enough time to enjoy the money you make.

The main thing is that your money is used to purchase experiences that are meaningful to you and that bring you pleasure... not just simply spent on things that society finds valuable.

Work and Career Prosperity

According to the "World Happiness Report", it is suggested that work-life [harmony] is a strong predictor of one's happiness, as well as job variety and the level of autonomy enjoyed by the employee. Job security and the support one receives from colleagues also have an impact on happiness. So, if you're unhappy with your work and career, then you're no doubt dealing with the negative effects in other areas as well.

You only need a paradigm shift on how you coordinate your work and manage your career to experience a harmonious life.

Spiritual Wellness

Spiritual Wellness is about understanding and embracing your true self. We put on different masks as our outward faces to the world, but too often, we forget to take it off again.

When we forget who we are and start becoming the masks we wear, that's when life starts feeling meaningless.

So "spiritual" isn't just about dedicating yourself to a religion — it's about understanding and aligning with your core values, beliefs, and ultimately your purpose. It's about staying true to yourself, finding your own purpose, and pursuing it. And it takes practice. A lot of it. Because we're too used to living in a world full of distractions.

Spiritual Wellness is essential for a life that seeks harmony and happiness. Studies have proven over and over again that having a healthy level of Spiritual Wellness can go very far in overall life satisfaction.

Mental Strength

The quality of your decision making and emotional regulation is anchored in Mental Strength.

The essence of Mental Strength is your attitude towards your fears, obstacles and challenges. This attitude is reinforced by developing skills that make you better at solving them, and giving you more and more confidence to face them head on.

With a strong mental baseline, you can find the opportunities in every obstacle, use creativity to solve problems, and see the importance of practicing lifelong learning. It's important to continually challenge your brain by learning new things regardless of your schedule.

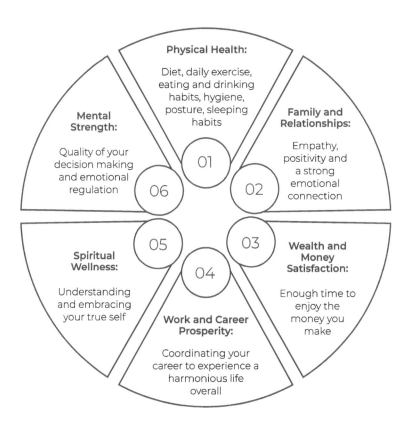

The Time to Live Fully is Now

> *"There are risks and costs to action. But they are far less than the long range risks of comfortable inaction."*
>
> —*John F. Kennedy*

Time is a non-renewable resource. Once it has passed, it cannot be replaced. This is why you should not squander time doing nothing, or delay certain decisions for later. More often than not, the biggest blocker from reaching our goals is often inaction — which is essentially doing nothing, rather than doing something.

There are many reasons why we may not do something, but often it boils down to not having the adequate time to accomplish said task. We may feel we don't have enough time due to other life obligations, or that it's never quite the right time to pursue our goals.

Maybe tomorrow, or maybe next year...

And, before you know it, more time has passed and you're nowhere near achieving those goals you put off. This inaction often leads to strong regret once the situation is looked at in hindsight. So, take some time now to reflect on any goal(s) you may have in mind, or even hidden at the back of your mind; and, consider the impact if you began working on them now, not later.

So, what is it that you're after in life?

A good amount of research has been done on the impact of having long-term and highly meaningful goals in our lives.

It is suggested that solidifying and following a purpose has connections to reduced stroke and heart attack. And, our desire to accomplish goals actually has an evolutionary connection—especially goals with a greater purpose to them. This is because a greater purpose often helps both the individual, and our species as a whole, to survive and thrive.

Knowing why you're doing something is also important, because it will be easier to budget your time and effort into pursuing milestones that will lead to the accomplishment of your main goal. Once you know what your main goal is, you'll want to make the most of the time you have. It's good to know how you're currently spending your time, so that you can start making improvements and easily assess what can stay and what can go in your day to day routine.

The bottom line is that we all have a very limited amount of time. Whatever your goals may be, the time to make them come true is not tomorrow, but right now.

You simply need to start. Don't let inaction waste any more of your time and leave you with only regret to show for it.

Lifelong Learning is the Key to a Fulfilling Life

"Develop a passion for learning. If you do, you will never cease to grow."

— *Anthony J. D'Angelo*

Don't we all want to live a fulfilled, happy and successful life? It often seems more like a fantasy rather than reality.

Many people believe that a "Full Life" is only possible if you're so rich that you don't have to worry about paying the bills or providing for your family. While having unlimited money certainly could make life easier, financial freedom isn't the answer to living a fulfilling life.

The truth is, anyone can pursue a life of fulfillment. It simply starts with the willingness to learn. And, learning doesn't stop when you get out of school. Beyond primary school, high school, and University, there is still so much out there to learn and experience; and this is the key to your true happiness.

It is true that a formal education and the resulting qualifications are important in securing certain jobs; but going to school is only one type of learning. All throughout your life, you're learning in many ways. All these experiences shape and grow you into the person that you are today and who you can become.

Lifelong learning is about creating and maintaining a positive attitude to learning both for personal and professional development. A lifelong learner is motivated to learn and develop because they want to; it is a deliberate and voluntary act. Lifelong learning can enhance our understanding of the world around us, provide us with more and better opportunities, and improve our quality of life.

No matter what stage of life you're in, being a lifelong learner brings its own rewards. It means we can get more personal satisfaction from our lives and jobs as we understand more about who we are and what we do. This can lead to better performance and a more rewarding work day. Whether it's for advancing your career, a personal interest or wanting to pursue new dreams, learning automatically pushes you forward towards progress and enhances your wellbeing.

Whatever your age, it's never too late to learn something new. When you begin exposing yourself to new knowledge and information, you widen your opportunities. This will allow you to do more than what you are currently doing, or it can provide you with an exit plan if you're not happy or fulfilled with where you're at now.

Lifelong learning goes beyond taking on new skills for your professional or personal development. It shapes your mind to be open to new perspectives and hidden opportunities. When faced with any setback or limitation in life, the key to change and finding your breakthrough lies within you. It's not your reality that's important, but rather your perspective of your reality. Therefore, being able to control how you look at things is the key to your breakthrough.

Enter the Full Life Framework.

Since all limitations start from your mind, it means that you can learn how to take control of the way you view your limitations. And, you can do so with the help of the Full Life Framework. By going through each step of this framework, you'll be able to transform your mindset and actions towards the change you need to achieve any goal you set your mind to.

So, what are you waiting for? The time to live a full life starts now.

The Full Life Assessment

We created The Full Life Assessment to help better understand where you currently are in life, so you know what to specifically improve upon to create harmony in all your Life Aspects.

It's important to note that I've included this Full Life Assessment in the first chapter of the book because I feel it is a critical first step in the Full Life Framework. I really encourage you to take the assessment before reading through the rest of this book. It will only take a few minutes of your time, and in return, you'll get a personalized breakdown of areas that you can improve on in your own life.

By taking this assessment, you will dig deeper into your own personal values and life missions and what creates meaning for you—and more importantly, establish where it is you want to go.

This assessment will help you understand the degree of balance you have in each of your Life Aspects and will help you determine any sacrifices you are currently making. This will help you grasp the methods I teach in the following pages and better understand how it relates to you on a personal level.

The knowledge you'll gain about yourself from the Full Life Assessment will better help you understand how to achieve a Full Life.

Follow this link to take the Full Life Assessment: https://www.lifehack.org/life-assessment-quiz

Tips for Success on Filling Out the Assessment:

1. Ensure you have at least 30 minutes of uninterrupted time to complete the assessment
2. Remove all distractions from the room (mobile phone, etc.)
3. Take 5 minutes to clear your mind before you begin
4. Answer each question honestly and thoughtfully; don't rush
5. Take 5 minutes to reflect on the assessment once you finish

#02

CHAPTER

Your Life Is a Mission

"You have to find what sparks a light in you so that you in your own way can illuminate the world."

— *Oprah Winfrey*

Do you know where you're going in life?

If you don't, you're likely to be forever drifting from one thing to another, like a log of wood in a stream – without making any genuine progress in your life.

Life is a mission and you are the driver. You are not just a log that drops from above and floats along with the currents of a stream. What makes you human is that you have agency to drive your own life. And agency results from Life Missions and having a main Life Purpose.

The first step is to consider your Life Missions. It's important to have one Life Mission for each of the 6 Life Aspects.

Remember, Life Missions work together in tandem to offer your life meaning, happiness, and most importantly, fulfillment. These missions are intrinsically driven, not from any external incentive. They are what get you up in the morning and motivate you to reach your goals.

Your Life Missions will influence your habits, choices, and goals, and provide you with a sense of direction. And, each of these missions will impact one another.

For example, running Lifehack is my main Life Mission for Work and Career, but it also impacts each of the other 5 Life Aspects. Thus, it is crucial to have a mission for each of your 6 Life Aspects so you can ensure they are all working in harmony.

As you progress through life, you will encounter several challenges that may shift your focus off of a particular Life Mission. But, rest assured, that change is inevitable, so it's actually a good thing!

Embracing Your Obstacles

Imagine for a moment you live in a utopian world where you never have to encounter adversities, blockers, setbacks or failures.

Sound like the perfect existence?

Not quite.

A world without obstacles would be a stale and lifeless world--one where you'd never be challenged, and one where you'd never grow. You see, obstacles can give us wonderful opportunities - providing we approach them with the right mindset.

And, obstacles in life are inevitable. Even if you locked yourself away in a room for a week, you wouldn't be able to escape from facing obstacles. For example, you might run out of food or water, you might be disturbed by noisy neighbors - or you might even develop cabin fever!

The good news is that you don't have to spend your life trying to avoid obstacles. Instead, you should anticipate them and deal with them head on. By doing this, you'll be able to transform obstacles into valuable opportunities for self-growth.

Whatever the obstacle you face, look for ways to overcome it and learn from it.

Whether it was in your past, or you're presently facing an obstacle, we all have to deal with them. Though unpleasant, these obstacles that come our way are necessary for growth. If we never had to face any adversities, blockers, setbacks or failures in life, our experiences would be cake! We'd have it so easy.

The downside? We would never be forced to adapt and mature.

So, in theory, having to face obstacles in life is actually desirable. The more obstacles you've faced, the greater the likelihood that you are quite mature and adaptable.

Though, not everyone tackles obstacles enthusiastically and head-on. Some people go to great lengths to avoid them... or go into denial about their existence. And, others let obstacles overwhelm them, and they feel defeated.

Most think of obstacles as a negative; but, if you can maintain an opportunistic attitude when facing your obstacles or limitations, you'll have an even more impressive result once you finally reach your goals!

Now, think about what obstacles are currently in your way.

What might you be faced with? Often, it's time and/or money limitations.

Here's an example:

Let's say you've always dreamed of writing a book—you find yourself daydreaming about the possibility (and have practically written 2 chapters in your head). The problem is, after work and family obligations, you definitely don't have enough time to write. You wish you could just quit your job to pursue writing full-time, but you also need money to pay your bills.

It's definitely not easy having to be in such a predicament. Most of us simply cannot drop our current routine to pursue something totally different.

But, you can do both!

What I mean is, you won't reach your goals overnight; but, you can take progressive steps towards them using your obstacles as a guide for your path.

In this case, you have to keep making income, and writing a book doesn't pay... so, your first challenge is to find a way to make money that will get you closer to writing. Or, you can find a way to increase your time.

One option is to find a job within your field that has more writing responsibility, which will position you well for writing your book, as you'll gain experience and better understanding of the writing world. Through your own career, you may get closer and closer to becoming a professional writer, which is excellent leverage when it comes to getting paid to publish a book.

Or, you could find just 60 minutes a day to dedicate to writing your book, and maybe get rid of something else you habitually do—such as streaming Netflix or playing video games. Those 60 minutes a day will add up and you'll be making major progress towards your goal.

Here are a few great reasons that I encourage you to start embracing your own obstacles, starting today.

Obstacles Make You More Confident

Sometimes obstacles can reset your objectives.

You might have always had a particular way of doing things, or wanted to pursue certain goals; but when you're faced with setbacks or difficulties, you're forced to re-think, and re-examine your path. And, you may end up focusing on something new and exciting—maybe something that you otherwise wouldn't have if not for the particular set back.

Granted, your obstacle may throw you off track for a bit, but it will also help you find strength when you're faced head-on with a challenge. By having to overcome an obstacle, you'll be proving to yourself that you are capable of overcoming difficult situations.

After you've overcome an obstacle, you're more likely to feel confident to overcome the next one that may come your way, and well prepared to tackle other goals ahead.

Obstacles Prepare You for the Unexpected

Even though obstacles aren't pleasant, they don't actually prevent us from reaching our intended goals. They serve as guides for where to go next, and—in a way—gives you time to stop and think if perhaps there is a new and better path to take.

While, of course, obstacles can bring out many negative emotions in us, such as frustration, anger, or sadness, it's important to realize that they don't inhibit us from reaching our destination – they only change the path we were originally expecting to take.

Obstacles Shift Your Perspective

Obstacles, whether we like it or not, are inevitable. Life is ever changing, and so we need to constantly change and adapt to new situations.

Life will never stop throwing you new obstacles. So, the best thing to do is know how to better see and deal with these obstacles, and transform them into opportunities for self improvement.

Everybody faces different obstacles – some much more severe than others. A few lucky people float through life with relatively few obstacles, most others face more difficulty. If you think of life like a game of poker, it's easy to see how it's advantageous to play the cards you're dealt to the best of your ability.

While inevitably some people are dealt better hands than others, your chances of success are mostly determined by how you play the game.

The more you're able to see obstacles as being an advantage to your life, the better you'll be at managing them and using the experience to propel you further. To successfully overcome adversities and reach your goals, you have to embrace the obstacles that come your way.

You certainly don't have to celebrate or welcome them with open arms, but rather accept and believe that these obstacles will push you to be stronger, help you grow and mature, and shape you to be more resilient. Your attitude towards setbacks will define the outcome of whether you rise from the challenge, or remain stuck in it.

Life is too short to be filled with staleness, defeat and disappointment. So go forward from this day with a positive attitude that enables you to benefit from obstacles that come your way. You'll feel happier and healthier. And in time, you'll begin to fall in love with the opportunities that obstacles give you.

Now, let me share with you a story about an obstacle that I never dreamed would get in my way: having a baby! I always assumed that if you are financially able, and emotionally capable, then having children would be... well, easy.

I'm sure many of you who have your own kids can see where this story is going. I quickly learned that it wasn't so easy!

...And Then My Son Was Born

A little while after I dedicated my career to Lifehack, I became the proud father to a new baby boy. He was amazing in every way, and my wife and I were so happy and excited to welcome him into our world.

And, I was excited to be bringing my son into a world where I was fulfilling my own dreams, that of which he could reap the rewards. Lifehack was gaining wider readership with millions of readers each month. My team was expanding and things were going great... that is, until reality set in.

My marriage started facing unexpected trouble once the baby was born. Turns out, it was pretty difficult juggling between my responsibility as a father and as CEO of Lifehack. And, unfortunately, my wife and son were at the receiving end as I simply wasn't present enough in their lives. And, due to the added stress, I also started really neglecting my self-care.

I made excuses, which resulted in actions that caused further stress:

- I felt guilty exercising because I should be spending that time with my family.
- I began working even more to prove to my wife that I was doing everything I could to support her and our son.
- I started eating a lot of junk food because it was so convenient to get a quick energy boost.

Clearly, I wasn't experiencing harmony in all the 6 Full Life Aspects. Now, I was sacrificing again, just in other areas.

This time around I was experiencing career satisfaction; but, the more successful I became, the more my other aspects in life suffered. An increase in my work success was creating distance from my family and a hard hit to my health.

I was getting pretty nervous about my future once again because my marriage was under considerable tension. After all, my wife was the primary caregiver of our son and she took care of the portion of housework I was neglecting--and with a new baby, that housework comes at you fast!

I wanted to be more present with my family, but my work at Lifehack was critical for us to maintain the unexpected expenses of having a growing family; and I made the mistake of thinking that by dedicating more time to work and earning more income, I would be able to pull us out of this new rut.

I knew the importance of balancing all Life Aspects, otherwise everything will go out of whack. And that's exactly what happened.

I felt overwhelmed in every area of my life, and my lifestyle habits were also complicating the situation. I was gaining weight, I was exhausted all the time, and my mindset was not healthy. Stress and anxiety was a normal occurrence, which didn't help communication with my wife.

At that point, I realized enough was enough; I needed to get real and start practicing what I preached. There's an inseparable connection among all Life Aspects. There was no way I could become successful in my business if I had to sacrifice my health and my family. Even if just temporarily, neglecting these aspects would eventually come back to haunt me.

So, I challenged myself.

I looked for means of transferring the skills that brought me success with Lifehack to all of the other aspects of my life. I couldn't sacrifice ANY area, or as time and experience has shown, it won't work.

It's much like trying to build anything without having all the necessary parts. Think about a piece of furniture you purchase from IKEA. What if some of the parts were missing? It would likely be impossible to build.

And, you also need the right tools, or else you struggle to make progress.

It's really as simple as that. Think of your own life like a neatly packaged piece of furniture you need to assemble. If you're not accounting for ALL the right parts and tools, you're going to face incredible challenges to accomplish your goal--and you may give up.

So, just like a piece of IKEA furniture, you need to have all the parts defined and right in front of you. These are the 6 Life Aspects.

And the tools, you can think of as Life Multipliers. I'll go more into detail on those later in the book.

So, the lesson in my story is simple:

It is critical to always re-evaluate your framework and adjust your methods or devise new strategies that align with any changes that come about. When it comes to my life, I may compromise my methods, but not my missions.

Do you know why it's challenging to stick to your Life Missions?

It's because change is unavoidable, and possibly scary at the same time. Every life is a series of changes that occur from birth to death. Change is the only fuel that enables one to survive and grow.

Perhaps you are presently afraid of making a wrong decision if you embrace change. You could be scared you might fall flat on your face if you change. Maybe you are not even comfortable with embracing a new belief system or adjusting to it. You may be torn between your old mindset and a new mindset, such as this Full Life Framework.

Your internal alarm system may be warning:

"What if I fail?"

And your mind may be clogged with things that hinder you from embracing change. But, change is on your side! Change can empower you to uncover your unexplored capabilities. You can't stop change from taking place. But *your response to change will determine your overall life experience.*

For me, I knew if I could apply the same skills that made me successful with Lifehack in a holistic way that addressed every single Life Aspect, I could overcome any obstacle that could come my way.

Change is beyond your control. Rather than striving to manipulate the circumstances, use the Full Life Framework to help guide you through the inevitable changes in your life that will come. You can easily lose your guard when you are in a transitional phase. Sometimes you may feel like you have lost your balance, or are out of control.

When you are facing obstacles or life challenges, it is easy to blame your spouse or someone else for not understanding enough.

I recall saying to my wife as she confided in me that she needed me to be more present in our marriage and with our son:

"Don't you understand I need to make more money to keep the family running?"

The truth is that it's tempting and sometimes seems easier to make excuses. But, these excuses will only complicate, or completely knock you off track of your mission. Yet, if you can show a positive perspective, such as seeing the lessons from those situations and the value of obstacles, then you'll find it much easier to embrace any change that comes.

Limitation only exists in your mindset. Your possibilities become boundless when you can learn how to view your boundaries from a positive perspective.

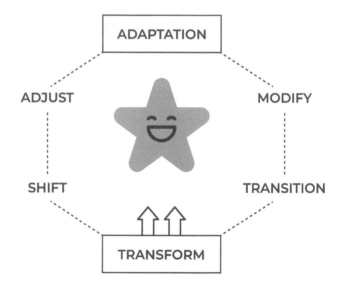

Defining Life Missions

Basically, everything we teach at Lifehack is related to the vitally important topic of Life Missions.

As you might recall from my personal story, it was only when I discovered that everything is tied together that I began to see success. By this, I mean, success comes from tending to all areas of my life at one time. This is a Full Life mindset.

Before I found and followed my life purpose to change people's lives for the better I was at least 80% focused on earning money. In fact, my career was driven exclusively by this factor. However, as I've outlined earlier, I paid a heavy price for putting my focus on wealth building.

Luckily, my discovering Life Aspects and Life Missions put me firmly back on track!

And it can do the same for you.

But before I show you how to find and follow your unique Life Missions, let me say a few words about the importance of having a Full Life mindset.

I'm sure you'd agree with me: life needs to be worth living! But what makes a worthwhile life? Well, principally, things that give meaning to our lives.

Let me give you an example:

Imagine you had a deep love of music, and when you were at school you learned to play several instruments, including piano and guitar. As your musical skills and experience developed, you joined a band. This band was not only fun and enjoyable to be part of — but you also had some success, including playing to large audiences and recording several songs.

However, as the band members reached college age, many went to different places to study, and the band was no more.

It was a sad loss for you, but you decided that music was never going to pay the bills, so you put down your instruments and instead focused on your college studies. You wanted to do well so that you could have a solid and safe career.

Years later, however, you found that office life was not the life you expected it to be. You hated the set hours, the menial tasks, and the general lack of creativity. You were like a fish out of water!

This nagging feeling that you were going in the wrong direction in life eventually motivated you to make some changes to your life. And the first of those changes was to pick up your musical instruments again.

They felt natural to you. And it felt great to be playing again!

After a few weeks of practicing at home, you decided to see if there were any bands looking for an electric guitarist. It didn't take you long to find one, and it was just a few weeks later that you made your debut gig with them — more than 15 years since you last played to an audience!

Suddenly, with your rekindled musical passion, your life seemed so much brighter and much more positive. Even your office job seemed less of a chore. You now had a hobby that was your pride and joy. A genuine life-changer.

Can you see from this short example how following your passion can transform your life?

And this was just by reintroducing a hobby. Imagine the type of transformation you could have if you changed your entire career or another major aspect of your life?

Finding your Life Missions is easier than you may think. It all starts with pinpointing the areas of your life that you are enthusiastic and passionate about. These could be a segment of your current professional role, a hobby, or even something you've only ever dreamed of doing!

Of course, it might not be smooth sailing...

For instance, when I first became a father, I saw how quickly my Life Missions were impacted. Of course, I don't mean this in a negative way. It was just that I had to quickly adapt to the very different circumstances I was experiencing.

This was when I realised that sometimes in our lives we have to compromise our methods — but not our Life Missions.

Compromise the Method, Not the Mission

Let me be clear:

True Life Missions should never be compromised, or this will create "debt" in our life — particularly of time, which is an invaluable resource we can never get back once spent.

However, it's possible (and oftentimes desirable) to compromise on your methods, without negatively impacting your Life Missions.

So how can you compromise your methods but not your Life Missions?

Well, the answer is to look at your mindset. If you take the mental approach that you'll probably have to drop one or more of your Life Missions — then that is likely what you will do.

But if you were to adopt a radically different mindset — namely, a positive one — you would be taking your first steps towards finding a workable solution to your problem.

I've said it before, and I'll say it again: *Success begins in your mind.*

"I'm going to figure it out no matter what" and "I'll find a way to overcome this!"

Thoughts like these will put you in a state of mental preparedness. And they'll give you the power to search for the answers you need. If you approach all your problems in this way, then you'll be driven to continually find ways to resolve them. But that's not all. You'll also find that — as a consequence of your positive attitude — you'll constantly make breakthroughs in your life.

At this point, you might be wondering to yourself what your personal Life Missions are.

Well, here are four questions to get you started on thinking about this:

- What kind of work do you want to do?
- What kind of parent/spouse/partner/friend do you want to be?
- What level of energy do you want to have?
- What do you really love doing?

Spend as much time as you need thinking about these questions. You may be surprised by some of your answers.

Remember: Each of your Life Missions play a meaningful and essential role in your life, and true success and happiness means fulfilling these missions.

And you don't need to just take my word for this, it's actually backed by science...

Dr. Alex Lickerman is an American physician, former assistant professor of medicine, and the author of two books: "The Ten Worlds: The New Psychology of Happiness" and "The Undefeated Mind: On the Science of Constructing an Indestructible Self". As you can imagine, to write these books, he had to undertake detailed research into the fields of psychology and mental health.

And what was his key discovery?

Having and following a life mission increases not only our happiness — but our resilience too.

Dr. Lickerman has also articulated a great way of honing in on your Life Missions. This is a six-step process that looks like this:

1. *Start with the right question.* Dr. Lickerman recommends this question: "What kind of value feels like the most important value I could create?"

2. *Look for meaningfulness not passion.* First discover what is meaningful to you. Passion will follow.

3. *Create a list of 100 things.* 50 that have brought you joy in the past; 50 that bring you joy in your life at the moment.

4. *From this list, identify the most meaningful items.* Go with gut feeling, but prioritize items that improve the lives of others.

5. *Then categorize these items.* Your categories might include: items that help people across the world (finding solutions to homelessness, for example); items that help people in an individual way (perhaps helping someone overcome their health issues).

6. *From these categories, write a first draft of your mission statement.* Dr. Lickerman's advice on this is to craft a mission statement based on experiences you've already had, not ones you'd like to have. The idea is to discover your mission — rather than inventing it.

Connecting Life Missions to the 6 Life Aspects

Okay, the next thing I'd like to talk about is how you can use the Full Life Framework to convert the 6 Full Life Aspects into 6 meaningful Life Missions. Before we get started, remember this: *Life Missions should fulfill a big fundamental inner desire in your life.*

Understanding the 6 Full Life Aspects is just the first step. That's because they're really categories that are designed to help you to evaluate your life from different perspectives. And everyone has different circumstances, as well as different requirements and needs in how they want to fulfill them.

Let me remind you... your life is unique!

There's no single path that everyone should just follow. Instead, you need to apply the 6 Full Life Aspects to make them meaningful to you. Do this, and you will create your own unique path that helps define success on your own terms.

This is where Life Missions come in. What are Life Missions?

Well, a mission is some sort of calling. So a Life Mission is a quest in your life that's meaningful to you. And it's the fulfilling of the mission (or missions) that gives your life a sense of purpose, significance and direction.

In other words, they're the things that make your life worth living — and what gets you out of bed every morning!

When you have the right Life Missions set, it will be easy to follow, as it will draw you towards them just like a powerful magnet effortlessly attracts metal particles. And your motivation to pursue your Life Missions will be sky-high. In fact, it will be like you're almost on autopilot!

No more need for punishments or rewards to motivate yourself.

Sounds good, right?

The secret is to convert what you want out of the 6 Full Life Aspects into meaningful Life Missions. Going back to the idea of super-motivation — meaningful Life Missions must fulfill a strong inner desire. What does this mean?

Well, put simply, an inner desire is basically something that deep down, you really, really want.

Think about it. Whenever you take any action in your life, it's because you're trying to satisfy some sort of need or desire. And when the desire is strong enough — you'll do whatever it takes to achieve it.

For example, when you go shopping for new clothes, you might believe that you're just choosing something that suits you or fits your budget.

But look a little closer, and you'll see that you're actually choosing clothes that express your personality, build your confidence, and show you off in the best possible light. If you didn't care about any of these things — you'd probably only go clothes shopping once a year!

Clearly, looking good is important for many people. And so you could say keeping up appearances is an inner desire for them.

Now, admittedly, that is a fairly small inner desire. When it comes to your Life Missions, you should seek to find your BIG fundamental inner desires.

I guarantee that you'll have at least one inner desire for each of the 6 Full Life Aspects.

To find out what they are, you need to ask yourself questions that dig deep into your inner self.

For example, on the surface a person may want to lose weight and get fit. But losing weight is just an outcome, and not really an inner desire. Let's face it — most of us don't find the idea of going on a diet and working out as particularly desirable!

But dig a little deeper, and you'll discover their real desire behind losing weight...

It's the same as my clothes example: They want to feel more attractive and have more confidence--or they want to feel more energetic and healthier. But whichever way you look at it, the losing weight part is the outcome, and the inner desires are the benefits I've listed above.

Those inner desires are what really motivates the person.

So as you can see, to discover your inner desires — you need to be 100% honest with yourself. A lot of people struggle because they're not really sure why they're doing something. Sometimes, they might be doing something for the sake of another person's inner desire.

The secret is that you need to take a step back and try to understand yourself.

Although this might sound a little scary, don't worry, as it's really just part of taking a path to self-discovery. A path you can walk slowly along, or one you can sprint down! It's your path; and you're in control.

Before I wrap up this chapter, let's take a look at the types of questions you can use to help you discover your Life Missions.

For example, the Full Life Aspect — Physical Health.

Just wanting to be "healthy" or "fit" isn't specific enough. You've got to pinpoint exactly what you want Physical Health to help you achieve.

You could start by asking yourself these questions:

- Why is physical health important to me?
- Which parts matter to me most? My fitness? My energy? My mobility? Or something else?
- What will superb physical health enable me to do? And what would happen to me if I lost it?
- What does success in this area look like for me? And where am I now compared to that?

The same goes for other Full LIfe Aspects, like Family & Relationships.

- What relationships will always matter to me now and for ever, no matter what?
- What kind of partner do I want to be?
- What kind of parent do I want to be?
- What kind of communicator do I want to be?

These are just a few examples of the questions you can ask yourself. I'm sure you can think of many more.

The next step — which is an important one — is to define your Life Missions based on the answers you have come up with for these questions.

To help you out, here's a real example of a Physical Health Life Mission from a colleague at Lifehack who's also a dad:

"I want a fit and active body so that I can always be there with my kids to play sports, swim, and explore the outdoors together. These are our most valuable bonding moments."

Now that's a mission that evidently comes from the heart. Driving him to stay healthy isn't himself — it's actually his children.

This is the way that Life Missions give you clarity.

But please remember, the missions you define right now don't have to be perfect. Don't waste your time on perfect mission statements with perfect sentences (and remember, perfection doesn't actually exist). Instead, let your mission statements be simple and concise, so that you can evolve and clarify them as you go along.

Life is a flow... and nothing is set in stone.

For instance, the dad's kids will grow up one day — and his Life Mission related to them will inevitably evolve.

The important thing is that your Life Missions are meaningful and motivating to you right now. When you read them, they should spark your attention and fire up your passion.

Time for Reflection

Now, it's your turn to discover what motivates you and find out your Life Mission for each of the 6 Life Aspects with the following brainstorming questions:

Physical Health

There's no denying the fact that you need to rely on your body — your strength and energy to do the things you need to do.

Why is my physical health important?

```



```

What does it enable me to do?

```



```

What would happen if I lost it?

```



```

What's most important to me in terms of physical health and why? (e.g. appearance, mobility, fitness etc.)

What kind of energy level do I want and why?

Therefore, my Life Mission for Physical Health is:

Family & Relationships Fulfillment

As social animals, having healthy and positive relationships help you grow and stay happy.

Why are my family and/or relationships important?

What do they enable me to do?

What would happen if I lost these relationships?

What's most important to me in terms of family & relationships and why? (e.g. my relationship with my partner, parenting my kids etc.)

What kind of person do I want to be in these relationships and why?

Therefore, my Life Mission for Family & Relationships Fulfillment is:

Work & Career Prosperity

A dream job or career is only a result. This Life Aspect is about how to get yourself on the right path to achieving that, and making sure it grows and stays meaningful.

Why is my work and career important?

What does it enable me to do?

What would happen if I wasn't happy with it?

What's most important to me in terms of work & career and why? (e.g. doing what I love, working with elites, leading a team etc.)

What achievements do I want at the end?

Therefore, my Life Mission for Work & Career Prosperity is:

Money & Wealth Satisfaction

Wealth and money are a means to an end. They help you achieve the things you actually want.

Why is money & wealth important to me?

What does it enable me to do?

What would happen if I lost my income?

What's most important to me in terms of money & wealth and why? (e.g. making as much money as possible, saving for retirement etc.)

Ideally, what kind of life do I want to live with my money and wealth?

Therefore, my Life Mission for Money & Wealth Satisfaction is:

Spiritual Wellness

True confidence and strength is built from a strong foundation of Spiritual Wellness. This matters to your direction and motivation.

Why is spiritual wellness important to me?

What does it enable me to do?

What would happen if I was spiritually unwell?

What's most important to me in terms of spiritual wellness and why? (e.g. feeling calm, mastering my emotions etc.)

What level of spiritual wellness do I want to have?

Therefore, my Life Mission for Spiritual Wellness is:

Mental Strength

This Life Aspect is how you face the outside world in the form of challenges and obstacles.

Why is mental strength important to me?

What does it enable me to do?

What would happen if I were mentally strong?

What's most important to me in terms of mental strength and why? (e.g. resilience, confidence etc.)

Ideally, how strong do I want mentally?

Therefore, my Life Mission for Mental Strength is:

Now you should have a better idea of what motivates you from the inside and what you actually find meaningful in life. So, what do you do with these Life Missions you've realized to live a Full Life?

You will need to invest and develop the right skills to improve different aspects of life. And to live the life you desire, it's more than acquiring the skills but utilizing them effectively.

The Benefits of Having a Purpose

In this chapter, I've talked a lot about Life Missions, and their importance to your health, happiness and success. However, there is one thing that you need to discover that is even more important than your Life Missions...

Your Life Purpose. This is your North Star. The thing that powers and determines everything you do in your life.

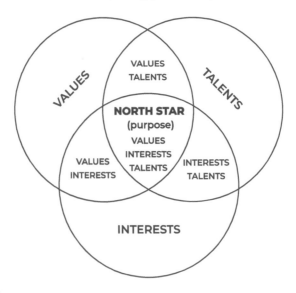

Before I show you some of the benefits of discovering and following your Life Purpose, let me ask you a couple of questions:

Do you know where you're going? And do you have a plan to get there?

If you've answered no to one (or both) of these questions, then I'm guessing your life is drifting from one thing to another, and you're failing to make any genuine progress.

There's a simple solution to this: a Life Purpose!

From my own experience, I can tell you that when you have something big to aim towards and — something for you to be genuinely excited about — your motivation will switch into turbo overdrive. Having a definite purpose in your life will bring you some incredible benefits. Let's look at four of these now:

Benefit #1: You'll Feel Braver and Stronger

What is one of the biggest fears in most people's lives?

It's the fear of not knowing what's going to happen next. This fear can be so paralyzing that for some people it can literally stop them in their tracks. This is where having a definite purpose can be a huge help. Once you've worked out what you really want in your life, you can plot your route to get there. This will not only set you up for lifelong success and achievement — but it'll also decrease the unknown and unleash your hidden strength.

You'll have drive. You'll be excited. You'll feel super-confident!

And these are traits that you won't have if you're currently drifting through your life.

So let's get straight to it: what exactly is a Life Purpose?

Well, I'd describe a Life Purpose as finding what you really enjoy doing and what you're naturally productive at.

Some people refer to a Life Purpose as a 'calling'. But whatever the label — it's vital that your Life Purpose contributes positively to society. When it does this, it will magically bring you an intense sense of satisfaction and achievement.

Your Life Purpose will also provide meaning to your life. And with this solid foundation, you'll develop the mental tools you need to face the ups and downs in life that you'll inevitably encounter on the way to reaching your goals.

The power of knowing where you're going and what you're aiming for also has another benefit: your fears will dissipate, and your courage will grow.

Benefit #2: You'll Give Your Health a Boost

Have you thought about the positive well-being effects of finding and following your Life Purpose? I recommend you do. As experience shows that a Life Purpose can improve your physical health — and give your mental health a boost, too.

A recent study published in The Lancet confirmed this. The study looked at how our attitude to life affects our happiness, health and longevity. The eight-year study of people with an average age of 65, found that those with the highest well-being were 30% less likely to die over the study period, living on average two years longer than those in the lowest well-being group.

Professor Andrew Steptoe, Director of the UCL Institute of Epidemiology and Health Care, who led the study, said:

"We have previously found that happiness is associated with a lower risk of death. These analyses show that the meaningfulness and sense of purpose that older people have in their lives are also related to survival. There are several biological mechanisms that may link well-being to improved health, for example through hormonal changes or reduced blood pressure."

The study also found some surprising health benefits of having a Life Purpose — such as an increase in walking speed over time. This effect was the equivalent to the purpose-driven participants being 2.5 years younger!

Imagine that.

While more research is needed, it's clear that having a sense of meaning and a Life Purpose won't just boost your health — it will also help you live longer and happier.

Benefit #3: You'll Become a Time Management Master

Another key benefit of having a Life Purpose is the positive effect it'll have on the management of your time.

This is best demonstrated through an example: Imagine for a moment that you've discovered your calling — to be a psychotherapist.

This calling would be your major goal, but to get there, you'd have to accomplish several smaller goals.

These would be things such as:

- Finding a college program to enroll on
- Finding the funding to pay for your courses
- Ending or modifying your current work/
  study commitments
- Starting your courses
- Gaining work experience
- Passing your courses
- Passing licensure exams
- Looking for work
- Starting your first job

Now, please take another look at that list.

As you may have noticed, It's actually an ideal roadmap to accomplish your major goal of becoming a psychotherapist. And it also conveniently breaks down the necessary steps into bite-sized chunks — making it simple and time-efficient to achieve each of them.

As I've mentioned previously: *It's important to remember that time isn't an infinite resource for us.*

That's why having a Life Purpose scores highly in this area, as it will drive you to take specific steps at specific times. And compared to someone drifting aimlessly through life, you'll use time to your advantage.

Benefit #4: You'll Feel a Sense of Accomplishment

American motivational speaker and writer Denis Waitley once said:

"Winners are people with a definite purpose in life."

I always like to remember that. And I hope you will, too.

Now, think for a moment about some of the major things you've achieved in your life so far...

Perhaps graduating from college, securing your first job, getting promoted, learning a new language, and becoming a parent, etc. These achievements are sure to have given you a greater sense of purpose in your life, as well as boosting your health, happiness and self-confidence.

Now picture this: You've discovered your Life Purpose, and you've plotted a clear and definite route to get there. The first thing this will do for you is that it will put a rocket booster under your confidence and drive! And you'll feel super-energized to keep progressing towards your goal — as it will be something that means everything to you.

And as you travel along the road to your purpose, you'll begin to understand how failure and mistakes are all just part of the road trip! No one is perfect. And no journey in life can avoid the inevitable bumps in the road. But at the same time, once you have a Life Purpose that you're pursuing, you won't need to worry about the ups and downs. That's because your inner drive to achieve your purpose will overcome any and all difficulties that you face.

Now, coming back to gaining a sense of accomplishment...

You can magnify this by celebrating the successful achievement of all your minor goals as you strive towards your Life Purpose. So now you know some of the amazing benefits of pursuing a Life Purpose — and I hope you feel inspired to find and follow yours!

I've taken you on a tour of many things that might be new to you, including Life Aspects, Life Missions and your Life Purpose (aka your North Star).

Before I conclude this chapter, I want to share with you a few questions that are specifically designed to help you think about your Life Missions in different areas of your life.

Please take as much time as you need to think about each question. This is an important exercise that could be the catalyst for major transformations in your life.

Think back to your Full Life Assessment, and ask yourself these questions:

- Have I discovered areas of my life that I'd like to change?
- What do I want to keep the same in my life?
- What am I currently spending time on that I'd like to focus less on?
- What can I NOT afford to lose?
- How would I define my own North Star?

You may find that your answers to these questions flash into your mind; or you may find that you have to spend hours or even days thinking deeply about the questions before you gain a clear perspective on your position.

Either way, I'm sure you'll find that these questions will lead you to life-changing answers.

So, are you ready to learn more?

In the next chapter, I'm going to help you to understand the value of something I like to call the Progress mindset. Briefly, this is a mindset that focuses on the efforts you invest into what you're trying to achieve. In other words, the progress you're making.

To give you an example of this, think of a complex project document that you need to write as part of your job. You could put your thoughts and how difficult this is, how much time it's taking and how painfully dull it is! Alternatively, you could focus on how the document will help your team/organization, how the document will help with your project presentations, and how it will impress your manager!

The first mindset is limited and restrictive, and will make completion of the document difficult and troublesome. The other one — which adopts the Progress mindset — focuses on the ongoing benefits of completing the document.

I'll talk more about this shortly.

The other thing I'm going to show you in the next chapter, is the power of progress-based goals.

This little-known technique asks you to throw away what you may have previously learned about goal setting. Instead of picking goals with specific endpoints (such as: I will earn an extra $10,000 this year), progress-based goals teach the principle of continually striving. You may hit the $10,000 dollar target, or you might go well beyond it.

Progress-based goals are non-restrictive. They allow you to flow with your life's momentum.

Interested in learning more about progress-based goals and the Progress mindset? Then read on!

#03 CHAPTER

The Progress Mindset

"There are only two ways to live your life. One is as though nothing is a miracle. The other is as though everything is a miracle."

– Albert Einstein

In the previous chapter, I covered the importance of Life Aspects and Life Missions.

These allow you to create desirable goals that are achievable and well within your reach. They also tie-in to the bigger picture — your Life Purpose.

And when you have all three of these things in place, you'll have an unstoppable forward momentum that will take you wherever you want to go, and enable you to be the person you really want to be.

No more pretence; you'll finally be living the life that you've always dreamed of.

With that tantalizing thought in mind, let's dive into something that I'm sure you're going to find fascinating: the Progress mindset.

The Key to Lifehack's Explosion:
A Progress Mindset

As you'll recall from the intro of this book, Lifehack began as a one-man show — and that one man was me.

At the time, I literally did everything... writing, editing, researching, publishing, marketing (to name but a few of my daily tasks). The first few months of going full-time was intense. Sometimes I would work 18-hours days — and sometimes these would become 20+ hour days!

But my hard work and persistence paid off, as the readers and subscribers to my site gradually increased.

This is what allowed me to expand my team with like-minded people who shared a passion for helping others improve their lives.

To be honest, it was strange at first having colleagues again. I had become used to working on my own, and making decisions on my own. Now I had a team, and as it grew, I needed to start thinking less like a one-man show and more as a CEO.

My time and energy was stretched so thin that I couldn't afford to spend time handling each situation on a one-off basis.

For things to take off, I needed to make each and every action lay the foundation for the next.

It was around this time that I had an epiphany.

For Lifehack to continue to grow and spread its message of hope and transformation, I needed it to be embedded with the principle of progress.

I remember when this insight came to me, that it felt intuitively like the right thing to do. And I wasted no time in drawing up plans on how to instill the power of progress into all areas of Lifehack.

My plan included:

- Putting learning and creativity at the forefront
- Fostering compassion for problems and people
- Integrating technology and human resources to achieve super-productive work outputs
- Adapting our content to the ever-changing life environment
- Fostering the strengths of my team members

To this day, this continuous progress ethos has been at the heart of everything we do at Lifehack. In fact, I believe it to be one of the main reasons for Lifehack's huge success.

One of my favorite quotes on progress is from Benjamin Franklin:

"Without continual growth and progress, such words as improvement, achievement, and success have no meaning."

The power of progress wasn't the only success secret that we adopted at Lifehack.

From early on, we had the courage to experiment a lot and accept failure often. In other words — we weren't afraid to step out of our comfort zones and keep trying new things.

And guess what? It worked wonders. Which is why we still follow this philosophy today.

Another thing we've done for a long time is to put our focus on learning and evolving, instead of fretting over metrics and numbers that we can't control. When numbers become your primary focus, you'll be at risk of suffering from "analysis paralysis". This is where you become so lost in the process of evaluating and examining data that you're unable to make any practical decisions. (Stock traders and game players often fall victim to this.)

But when your focus is firmly on learning and progress, you'll worry less about the numbers, as your thoughts and actions will be directed to keeping you moving forward in life.

Thousands of readers became millions of readers.

That is the explosive growth we've seen at Lifehack since we applied the success secrets I've mentioned above.

Of course, there are other factors responsible for our success. But for now, I want to keep your focus on progress!

After more than a decade of leading Lifehack's dedicated team, I've had the opportunity to discover things that work and things that don't.

However — throughout the ups and downs — I've ensured that we've continually honed our strategies to align with our progress-based ethos. No matter how many times our methods have been compromised, we've stuck to our mission: to help as many people as possible change their lives for the better.

As a leader, I've always gone out of my way to encourage our team to do lots of:

- Testing and experimentation
- Progress-based goal setting
- Constant refinements of tasks and projects
- Acceptance and understanding of failures (which happen a lot - but we always learn from them!)

To give you an example of this, if we have a plan that is off track, I don't expect my team to stick to it until it is a proven failure. Instead, we work together to revisit and revise the plan until we find a formula that works. With every project, big or small, we chart our progress. This makes it easy to see at a glance what needs to be done to get the project over the line, or if we need to change direction.

We also organize weekly team meetings and weekly one-on-one meetings to continuously check in with the team.

In terms of technology, we are constantly seeking and implementing the optimum tools to do the job. And if any of our existing tools are no longer fit for purpose — we quickly search for and start testing new solutions.

Each of the team members have a distinct role and:

- Commitment to lifelong learning and improvement
- Commitment to personal health and wellness
- Full ownership of important tasks and projects
- Advice from outside experts to help with career development
- Regular encouragement and re-strategizing of individual strengths

In addition to the above, we offer remote working options to all our staff. This helps bring in talent from all over the world and provides flexibility to everyone who works for Lifehack. This approach is crucial in keeping Lifehack moving forward.

And, it's as simple as always thinking of the progress we are making. Encouraging the best from my team — including supporting them outside work life — is integral to their success, and the success of the company. Now you've seen how we do it at Lifehack—so why am I telling you this? Because you can do the exact same thing for yourself!

At the core of having a Full Life is adopting a Progress mindset.

STATIC MINDSET	PROGRESS MINDSET
My abilities and talents determine my success	My effort and attitude determines my success
I'm no good at solving problems	I can improve my problem solving abilities
When I hit an obstacle, I give up	When I hit an obstacle, I see it as an opportunity to take a different path
Every time I fail, it proves I'm not good enough	Every time I fail, I learn something very valuable
When someone else succeeds, I feel threatened	When someone else succeeds, I feel inspired
I've done the best I can	Is this really the best I can do?

Defining a Progress Mindset

So what exactly is a Progress mindset?

Well, it might help you to know that it is sometimes referred to as a "Growth Mindset".

I'll start by explaining the opposite mindset — something you could refer to as a Static Mindset.

This is the mindset that most people have (at least about some aspects of their lives). And it manifests in thoughts like these:

- I'm not a creative person.
- I think school was the best days of my life.
- I'm happy with the status quo.
- I'm too old to learn new things.
- I don't need the stress of a promotion; I'm waiting for my pension!

Now, don't get me wrong. I'm certainly not judging. In fact, I recall having many of these exact thoughts myself. But when you look at the list above, I'm sure it becomes clear to you how someone with a Static mindset thinks and acts. They've lost interest in progress. And instead, they're stuck in a world of constantly trying to keep things as they are.

And worse than that, they start to believe the falsehood that our character, intelligence, and creative ability are static givens which we can't be changed in any meaningful way. Now, let's compare that with someone who has a Progress mindset.

Their thoughts will look something like this:

- I'm always seeking new experiences.
- I focus on solutions, not problems.
- I have an open-mind and positive outlook.
- I never want to stop learning.
- The best years of my life are still to come!

As you can see, the owners of a Progress mindset are constantly seeking opportunities to grow; and their mental door is always open to opportunities. These are individuals who believe their talents can be developed through hard work, effective tools, getting outside of their comfort zone and accepting input from others.

The Differences Between a Progress Mindset and a Static Mindset

Digging deeper, you'll find these mindsets to be different in all manner of things. This is a person's way of thinking and viewing the world. When we change how we view things, our entire lives change. Consider these differences.

1. Differences in Challenges

The first aspect is how they approach challenges.

People who have a Static mindset will do everything they can to avoid challenges in their life. If there is an easier solution, they'll take it. Some examples of this are things like not studying for a test because they're not good at the subject. Or only doing specific tasks at work that they know they can do with little issues or discomfort.

On the other hand, those with a Progress mindset embrace challenges in their lives. Yes, some of the work or effort may come out short, but they understand failure is part of learning. What matters to them is that they have tried their best in those moments. After that, they learn and grow from the experience.

2. Differences in Handling Feedback

Next is how each one handles feedback and criticism.

For those with a Static mindset, they will react in a knee jerk negative way. Some will harbor disdain while others will ignore or avoid it as much as possible.

For those with a Progress mindset, they view these talks as opportunities to grow. While it's about their work and efforts, they don't see it as an attack on their abilities. Provided that the criticism is valid, these individuals will take it to heart and incorporate it into their lives.

3. Difference in Intelligence

In particular, the belief of intelligence.

As I mentioned above, a Static mindset is fixed. So with a Static mindset, when it comes to intelligence, you either have it or you don't.

On the other hand, someone with a Progress mindset believes that intelligence isn't an inherent skill and can be developed. They believe that if they put in enough effort, things will move along and your intelligence can increase.

4. Differences in Tolerance

What I mean by tolerance is how long people can tolerate something before giving up or stopping.

For those with a Static mindset, giving up comes too easily. This shouldn't be much of a surprise as they like to avoid problems and challenges. Any sort of roadblock has the potential to destroy an entire goal.

Those with a Progress mindset though, are persistent and try harder. They're not ones to shy away from challenges. And even if they fail, they try again later.

5. Differences in Viewed Success

It's also worth looking at how those with a Progress mindset versus a Static mindset view success. For a Static mindset individual, they are often jealous of those who succeed in anything. Deep down though, these individuals experience self-doubt which comes from insecurity.

Compared to a Progress mindset individual, they get inspired by seeing others succeed. In many cases, they even help others around them succeed. That's because they believe in themselves and feel they can help others, too.

6. Differences in Failure

To no surprise by this point, those with a Static mindset will shield themselves from failure. If they ever experience it, it's often a negative experience. In fact, many people get stuck on one failure for their entire life. It's as if one failure has barred them from ever putting in effort into that area again.

But those with a Progress mindset don't have the word "failure" in their vocabulary. They see these as setbacks or opportunities to learn. They're more eager to learn from their failures and are willing to grow as a person.

7. Differences In Learning

Attitude about learning also is a key difference.

For those with a Static mindset, they stop learning at some point in their lives—often after University. They think that the learning ends after that point and you have to use that knowledge for the rest of your life.

Those with a Progress mindset understand the truth. They know industries, people, and the world changes around them. We live in an information age where more information is being put out every day. They recognize that learning doesn't stop after University. It's only starting.

8. Differences In Confirmation

For those with a Static mindset, they need to prove to themselves and to others that they are valuable. It's akin to our kids posting on social media for validation. Their attitude about themselves is judged by how many likes or comments they get.

It all boils down to numbers. For those with a Progress mind set, this aspect doesn't exist. Sure there is some confirmation, but it stems from internal thoughts rather than from external sources.

9. Differences in Effort

While this is an obvious one on the surface, there is more to it than that. After all, a mindset is developed through events and how we interpret those events in our lives.

For the Static mindset, while they will do anything to avoid any negative events, that desire stems from deeper beliefs. Yes, they think everything is a fixed level, but that belief stemmed from how they were raised.

In the end, those with a Static mindset believe that effort stems from their own abilities that they possessed already.

Compare that to a Progress mindset: their belief system is that effort stems from their willingness to develop something, or a result of failing at something and learning from those experiences.

A mindset shapes our view of the world and the people that are in it. When we change our mindset to that of progress, we clearly see the world in a different light. By developing yourself in this area and adopting this mindset, you too can change your life and grow more than ever.

It probably won't surprise you, but people with a Progress mindset tend to achieve more than those with a Static mindset. They're also likely to be happier and more satisfied with their lives. So which mindset would you like to have?

Mindset Matters

As I have covered, it's vital that you adopt a Progress mindset if you want to live a healthy, happy and successful life. It's the difference between being stuck in a harbor or sailing out on the open sea!

STATIC MINDSET	PROGRESS MINDSET
GIVE UP	GOALS
STOP	FULL LIFE
FAILURE	SUCCESS
CAN'T	ADAPTATION
SHOULDN'T	COULD
FEAR	OPPORTUNITY

Personally, I'm always re-evaluating and improving my methods — but I never compromise on my Life Missions.

And one thing is for certain, there are always going to be obstacles. No matter what you do or what you plan for, obstacles will continually appear in our lives.

But, imagine if there was a way to break through these obstacles and transform them into turning points. That would be amazing, wouldn't it?

Well, the good news is that it's very possible.

Your Attitude Can Smash Through Walls

Every day, month and year we encounter problems and obstacles. And if we allow these to break our focus and destroy our confidence - then we'll quickly be defeated by life.

But if we can see these things as challenges to be overcome, then instead of feeling negative about them, we can look forward to finding ways to conquer them. And with this type of mindset, instead of obstacles blocking your way - you'll smash right through them!

Let me give you an example... Remember when you learned to ride a bike? Your first few attempts no doubt ended with you falling painfully onto the ground. Now, this could easily have led you to say: "No more!" "I don't want to hurt myself in this way."

But as you'd seen your friends and family effortlessly cycling and enjoying themselves, you were determined to keep going and learn the art of riding a bike. And it was this positive attitude that eventually led you to develop the necessary balance to successfully ride a bike and enjoy cycling.

This is the same attitude that you should take towards all obstacles that come your way.

Obstacles Are Inevitable, So Embrace Them

Once you realize that obstacles are inevitable, then you can start to embrace and overcome them.

But, how does one do this?

It all comes down to your mindset.

If you let obstacles easily defeat you, then you'll struggle to make headway in life. But, if you develop a Progress mindset that sees obstacles as opportunities, then you'll be well on your way to winning the game of life.

You could say that obstacles are the secret key to happiness.

They force you to understand new experiences, think of new ideas, and go outside of your comfort zone—but only if you approach them with a positive mindset, and remember the lessons you're learning, the wisdom you're gaining, and the better version of yourself that you're building.

Everyone who has achieved huge success in their lives (think Jeff Bezos, Richard Branson and Sheryl Sandberg) has also faced many failures. Nobody wins every time, which is why the ability to keep going in the face of adversity is a vital attribute if you want to make the most of your life. It may seem too simplistic, but with the right mindset, anything is possible. This means paying more attention to the positive side of things when challenges come your way.

For example, if you're battling with deadlines at work, don't see that as a bad thing. It means that you're in demand for what you do.

One great way to develop and reinforce a positive attitude is to always celebrate your wins, big and small.

And keeping a Progress mindset is key. The power of this lies in the fact that even when you encounter a difficulty, you'll be able to see from your tracking that - despite the current setback - you're still progressing onwards and upwards towards your goal.

Why Is Staying Inside of a Comfort Zone Bad for Us?

So why is it so bad for you to be staying in your comfort zone? Well, one thing that I've come to learn is that in order to improve, it's essential that you embrace fear and change in your life.

The issue with fear and change is that when we are comfortable, we are less inclined to make those changes and lean on our fear. In the end, your life will begin to stall and remain unchanged.

On the surface, this doesn't seem all that bad. However, with life, change tends to find a way. Whether it's through something large like COVID-19 or something smaller like you wanting to be a better partner, these shifts come with risks and changes.

And depending on how much we are determined to remain in our comfort zone will determine how much we resist those changes, even in situations where those changes are very good for us.

What Keeps Us from Stepping Out of Our Comfort Zone?

As I've hinted at a little bit, our resistance can stem from many places. That said, the most common ones can be boiled down to three fears:

- Fear of change
- Fear of failure
- Fear of the unknown

These fears are all manageable, and by learning about them, you can start to break them down in a way that works best for you. Here is what you can do for each one.

Fear of Change

As the most generalized fear of the three, this fear tends to mask the other two. You'll be able to tell because this fear often leads to thoughts like:

- This task is too big.
- Why me?
- I can't do this alone.
- I don't know where to start, so I won't do it.

As you can tell, if you have a fear of change, you'll justify it in order to procrastinate on whatever it is that you need to be doing. You would rather keep things the way they are than put in work and take risks. It's a natural feeling that you've likely been leaning on ever since you were a child. It's been ingrained in you. What matters now is that you work on changing it.

Fear of Failure

Going past fear of change, perhaps you remain in your comfort zone due to a fear of failure. I'm sure that many of you can relate as this particular fear can be instilled in various ways:

- A childhood event or upbringing can cause you to internalize damaging mindsets.
- You are a perfectionist or have perfectionist tendencies.
- You over-inflate failures in your head, whether they are in reality big or small.
- You are masking true confidence with false confidence when it comes to your personality and abilities.

Getting into more detail, fear of failure can be described as a lack of confidence in yourself and your current abilities to complete a task or goal.

Fear of the Unknown

The last common fear is the fear of the unknown. From a logical standpoint, this makes sense, too. Life is a mystery, and we have no idea where it'll take us. Instead of you seeing this as a gift, you may use that as a reason to be paranoid and afraid whenever there is something that would disrupt your way of life.

This disruption can be something major like a job loss to something smaller like getting into better shape.

How you react depends on who you are, but it always comes back to you resisting change out of worry that your life could be different or, at best, better.

How to Break Out of Your Comfort Zone

Now that you have an understanding of the potential fears that stand in your way, you need to learn to break them down. Regardless of what fear you have, the methods to pushing yourself out of your comfort zone are relatively similar. I say "relatively" because how people choose to act in order to succeed and strive in life varies from person to person.

It is important to remind yourself of some key aspects of change, which is the root of breaking out of your comfort zone. Change is a journey that you must take if you want to succeed. Part of that change is having lessons and learning from those lessons.

As many others have said before me, even if you fail, it's not a complete failure unless you didn't learn something. Learning is all a part of life, *and walking away with a lesson can be just as rewarding as achieving something.*

True Positivity

If the thoughts that run through your head are mostly negative, your outlook on life is likely to be gloomy and pessimistic. This is going to majorly impact your efforts to sustain a Progress mindset.

Conversely, if your thoughts are mostly positive, you're likely to be an optimist and see the sunny side of life and you'll find a Progress mindset comes more naturally.

Of course, positive thinking doesn't mean ignoring bad or unpleasant situations. It means that you approach unpleasantness in a more positive and productive way. Instead of taking everything as if you're a victim of negative circumstances, you see challenges and obstacles as an opportunity to learn and grow.

So how do you keep your mind on the positive? One of the best ways to do this is to be aware of self-talk.

By this, I mean the endless stream of unspoken thoughts that run through your head. These automatic thoughts can be positive or negative. Some of your self-talk comes from logic and reason. Other self-talk may arise from misconceptions that you create because of lack of information. Still others could come from external sources—such as negative people around you, or from media such as TV, movies, news, etc.

It's also important to be aware that positive thinking has proven health benefits including a significantly reduced risk of cancer and heart disease.

In addition to boosting your physical health, positive thinking can also:

- Lower your levels of stress
- Improve your psychological well-being
- Increase your coping skills during challenging situations

Clearly, positive thinking is essential if you want to adopt a Progress mindset and make some real headway in your life.

Be Grateful

Being grateful for your accomplishments and the support in your life will help you see them more clearly, build your own confidence, and give you a better outlook overall on what your limitations really are - and what you have to do to overcome them. It will set the stage for you to see the progress you're making in your own life, and have gratitude for it.

With a grateful attitude you'll be able to limit the damage of negative influences and strengthen the impact of positive ones. You'll be able to easily adapt a Progress mindset. You'll be able to set new, exciting goals - and achieve them!

You'll also find the inner strength to overcome adversities. This will create a positive snowball effect that will transform your physical and mental health, as well as enabling you to create the life you've always dreamed of. This is all truly something to be grateful for.

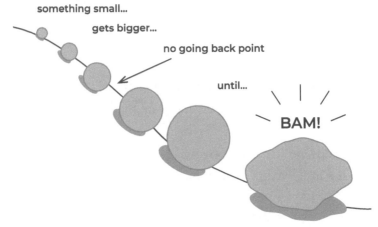

Don't Forget to Love Yourself

You can also help develop a Progress mindset by changing your perspective about yourself.

The same way your body needs nutrition to survive; likewise, your mind needs positive and encouraging words and images to stay healthy. Whatever you see or hear can affect your thought pattern and your overall well being.

Take charge of your mind by choosing what to believe. Think positivity and be sure to give yourself lots of credit!

Positive affirmations are a time-tested strategy to remind yourself always that you're in control. That you are worthy. That you are capable of so much.

Here's a few Positive Affirmations that I'd encourage you to repeat to yourself often. Write them down in a small notebook or store them in your notes on your smartphone. Set a reminder to read them every single day.

You can pin or tape these positive affirmations in strategic spots, such as your cubicle wall, your laptop screen, your phone screen, and around your house. This approach will enable you to monitor your thoughts and give you gentle reminders to keep going.

Daily Positive Affirmations

- I am the architect of my life; I build its foundation and choose its contents.
- I forgive those who have harmed me in my past and peacefully detach from them.
- Creative energy surges through me and leads me to new and brilliant ideas.
- Happiness is a choice. I base my happiness on my own accomplishments and the blessings I've been given.
- My ability to conquer my challenges is limitless; my potential to succeed is infinite.
- Today, I abandon my old habits and take up new, more positive ones.
- Though these times are difficult, they are only a short phase of life.
- My future is an ideal projection of what I envision now.
- My efforts are being supported by the universe; my dreams manifest into reality before my eyes.
- My obstacles are moving out of my way; my path is carved towards greatness.
- I wake up today with strength in my heart and clarity in my mind.
- My fears of tomorrow are simply melting away.
- I am at peace with all that has happened, is happening, and will happen.
- My life is just beginning.

Keeping a Progress Mindset

You can achieve real happiness and fulfillment in life when you pay attention to the progress you make in all your life aspects.

A Progress mindset is based on visible actions. These concrete actions will produce meaningful results that you can re-invest as your learning curve improves.

Here are a few ways to help maintain a Progress mindset.

Find a Mentor

Mentorship is essential to keep a Progress mindset. There's no growth in insolation. You need to learn from people who have gone before you.

Sometimes, you quickly get lost in your problems, and stray away from the path of positivity. A mentor can give you a reset so you can focus on your goals and develop a new perspective.

Look to Role Models

If you are finding it hard to discover your capability to make progress, look for friends and people in your network for evidence that diligence and consistent effort work.

If you continually think," He's born with those talents," change your mindset. Nobody came into this world with a Progress mindset; you have to learn a Progress mindset.

A role model can help you see what's possible and enable you to stick to your Life Missions. Their successes will be the evidence that your goals are possible.

Learn From Your Mistakes

Someone with a Static mindset will quickly succumb to the belittling voice in his or her head when an obstacle somes their way and may not learn from their mistakes.

Someone who holds a Progress mindset, however, will always look back and see what they can learn from their past experiences. This enables growth, which goes hand in hand with progress.

Don't Compare Yourself to Others

Ranking our success based on others' outcomes is something that many of us do. But I've discovered that it always produces a Static mindset. You have unique abilities. What matters is not how you compare yourself to others, but how you compare yourself to who you were yesterday. Are you making progress? If so, that's what counts.

So focus on your efforts instead of your outcomes. Never compare yourself with others. Only ensure you are making progress each day in line with your Life Missions.

Don't Be Afraid to Ask for Help

American businesswoman Rona Barrett said:

"The healthy and strong individual is the one who asks for help when he needs it."

She's absolutely right. But sadly, most of us are taught that asking for help is a sign of weakness. For example, we often avoid asking for directions when we're lost - in an effort to appear that we're still in control. This is despite the fact that asking for directions would actually be the correct action to take in this case. (Unless you enjoy going around in circles!)

When I started Lifehack, I initially thought I had all the answers. In fact, I was pretty arrogant in this respect - often turning down offers of help and advice from others. But it wasn't long before I realized the truth in the statement: "No man is an island."

I was only able to make the big breakthroughs with Lifehack when I listened to the advice of other successful entrepreneurs. And I also found it incredibly useful to have a business mentor. This was someone who I could call on regularly to ask for help with resolving issues, and for support in developing and implementing the best possible ideas.

If you've been conditioned at school or college (or both) to regard asking for help as a weakness, I urge you to shake this conditioning off! Asking for help from the right people will massively increase your confidence, success and influence.

And it'll also open up new doors of opportunity for you.

Setting Progress Based Goals

The most exciting thing about a Progress mindset is that you can make it practical by establishing progress-based goals.

A Progress mindset means you are viewing your life as a flow, and you are improving at working on your goals each day. You are making progress in all your 6 Life Aspects.

There's no such thing as overnight success, and if you're going to achieve anything significant in life, you have to take steps to get there. Everything is presently moving at a breathtaking speed. Technology is changing, and IT companies are releasing updates to keep up with the changing technology.

The truth is your life is also progressing at a breathtaking pace. Because of this, many of us want things to happen as soon as possible—for our lives to change immediately. But, this rarely happens. One thing that you CAN change immediately is your mindset—and focus on progress. When trying to make changes in your life or achieve set goals, always see your life as a flow instead of an event. You need to build on your small wins and victories to achieve the next bigger goals.

Small wins are a realistic, easy-to-attain, portion of your larger goal. This bite-size objective may vary based on the timeframe, desire, and specific intention.

The reason it's so effective is that you can see tangible evidence quickly, so you have this sense of fulfillment, and you are inspired to move on to the next mini-goal.

BIG GOAL
Too big, uncertain, scary

BITE SIZED GOALS
Small, immediate progress

Here are some instances:

If you want to lose weight, become fit, or live a healthy life, it is essential to establish intermediate milestones instead of focusing on a massive change. For instance, you can set a small goal of losing at least 5 pounds every month, instead of achieving 60 pounds in a year.

You can achieve this by replacing all soda with water or eating more whole foods over processed foods. Just one small step that makes progress is all it takes.

Having the 60 pounds weight loss goal above your head and trying to modify your entire lifestyle all at once can lead you to become overwhelmed and give up on your goals. But, if you have one goal, meet it, make it a habit, and then move onto the next, you'll be astounded at your results in no time!

Take that small step, then go for the next tiny target.

This is huge progress!

Achieving a mini-goal that is part of the big picture will provide you the victory, confidence, and the evidence that you can make the next goal. *Every small victory is the fuel that propels you to the finish line.*

Setting Goals

Several studies have found out that the ability to delay your immediate gratification and maintain a laser-focus on your goals is what determines success.

Here is the implication: successful individuals are not necessarily "smarter" than the rest of the world; they have only mastered how to set goals and focus on achieving them. So what do you do when you are failing at sticking to your goals?

Align your goal with your true intention or North Star. If you don't know what you want from life, you can never be committed to your goals.

How do you find your North Star? Ask yourself what you want from life, why you want it, and be honest with your answers. You can utilize the 5 Whys method to dig deeper into what you want.

The 5 Why Methods is a proven technique where you brainstorm which of the answers will bring you the best value. It helps you to generate significant responses.

Here's an example:

Lydia is a young mom who works long hours at a desk job, leaving her exhausted and with little time for physical activities. She recently joined a gym because she wanted to get fit.

If Lydia broke down her goal by asking the 5 Whys, she would find that her reasons for wanting to achieve her goal are actually directly related to her own North Star.

Lydia's 5 Whys for getting fit

What's my current goal? To work out for 30-60 minutes at 5 times per week.

- **Why do I want this?**
  Because I want to be more fit

      Why... do I want to be more fit?
      Because I am totally out of shape and don't feel good about my physical fitness.

      Why...?
      Because I don't make it a priority exercise and I am always exhausted after work

- **Why... is that a problem?**
  Because my son is turning 2 and I don't want to have difficulty keeping up with him.

- **Why... is this important?**
  Because I want to be actively involved in his upbringing and not feel bogged down both physically and mentally. I know that being physically fit will enable me to be a better mother for him during all his life stages.

In this case, the true intention of Lydia goes well beyond just "getting fit." It's to be a healthier role model and mother to her son. Which, coincidentally aligns with her North Star—to create a harmonious work life circle so she can spend more quality time with her son.

See how it all connects?

Now that Lydia can make the goal of working out about her relationship with her son, it becomes intrinsically motivating. It's easy to give up on your goals if they aren't aligned to your North Star. But, if they are, you'll find the motivation comes much easier. It's also helpful to use the SMART goal setting technique, which is outlined in the box below. It can help you narrow down your focus and priorities, to ensure your goals are reached.

SMART Goals

Use the SMART technique when establishing either long or short-term goals. In short, SMART goals are goals that hold each of these 5 aspects:

Specific

It's important to be able to state your goal clearly in specific terms. This way, you can make better plans and maximize your time and resources. It will also help you to focus on what's important.

For instance, the goal: 'I want to earn a good income' is not specific. Instead, say, 'I want to earn at least X amount from working at home.' Thus, you can learn high-income skills, which you can translate to skills for a specific job. This will enable you to focus and take small steps in the direction of your goal.

To set specific goals, ask yourself these questions.

- What exactly do I want to achieve?
- Who is involved?
- Where will it take place?

Measurable

You also need to be able to precisely quantify those goals. Use numbers instead of vague adjectives. At the very least, you'll want to know when you've achieved the goals.

For instance, using the previous example, say, "I want to earn $X monthly by working as a Digital Marketing Freelancer." You can make your goals measurable by asking yourself the following questions:

- What milestones do I need to meet to make progress?
- How much change needs to happen and by when?
- How many actions or accomplishments will it require?

Achievable

The main objective of setting a goal is to achieve it. There is no point if you can't attain your goals.

An achievable goal should align with the available resources and skills. If it factors in options that are beyond your control, then you cannot achieve it.

Ask these questions:

- Do I have, or can I get the resources needed to achieve the goal?
- Is the goal reasonable for me?

Realistic

Before you commit yourself to any goal, you need to determine if it is practical. It should connect to the world of reality. Not only that, but it should also complement your 6 Life Aspects. If you have to trade off different aspects of your life, then the goal is not worth it.

So ask yourself:

- Am I willing to make these commitments to reach the goal? Why?
- Are the actions I plan to take likely to bring success? Why?

Time-bound

Every goal must start on a specific date and end at a specified future day. That's why you need to divide your goals into milestones and establish deadlines. This will propel you into action.

With deadlines, you can quickly know if you are making progress or you are retrogressing.

"I want to start earning $X monthly by the end of next year" is a time-bound goal.

Remember, within this year, there are short term goals, mid-term goals, and long term goals. You simply need the small wins to stay motivated.

Ask yourself these questions to establish a time-bound goal:

- What is the deadline for reaching the goal?
- When do I need to take action?

You can only make significant steps towards a full life when you establish SMART goals that align with your true intention. You will face challenges. Just stick to your goals and boost your motivation by celebrating small-wins as you make progress.

How To Write Effective SMART Goals

Now that you have an in-depth understanding of what SMART goals are, you'll want to commit these goals to paper. Keeping them locked in your head might make sense, but if you don't write them down, you're not going to feel as compelled to complete them.

We have billions of thoughts over the course of the day, and sometimes having a written reminder for some things helps. However, when you get into writing, you'll find that there is more to writing these goals down than simply ensuring they hit the SMART criteria.

You'll find yourself asking more questions, and the answers will begin to adjust your goals further and your strategy to achieve them..

Another tip when it comes to setting SMART goals is that you want to be setting only one and working it through the SMART criteria. After that, you can consolidate the goal into one statement.

SPECIFIC	MEASURABLE	ATTAINABLE	RELEVANT	TIME BOUND
Make sure that your goals are clear and concise.	Make sure that your goal is not vague and is quantifiable.	Is your goal possible to be achieved?	Does it align with your North Star?	Make sure that your goal has a deadline.

You'll only want to set one goal because when we set multiple goals, it can create competition for our attention. Similar to how we shouldn't be multitasking, we don't want to set multiple goals for similar reasons.

It breaks our focus and can lead to more problems down the road. Instead, it's important that we set goals, achieve them, and then maintain the results as we progress towards other goals.

Setting a Progress-Based Goal

The key to setting a Progress based Goal is to ensure that it leans towards progress, instead of an outcome.

Here is an example of how an outcome-based goal can be changed into a progress-based goal:

Example #1:

"Create a morning and evening routine that guarantees I'm never tired in the morning."

This goal focuses on a specific result — whether you're tired or not in the morning.

By focusing on the outcome, it's harder to immediately see where to improve. What if you feel great the first few mornings, but on the fifth and sixth ones you feel tired? Then are you suddenly failing with the goal?

Looking at it this way will lead to lots of ups and downs, leaving you discouraged and losing momentum.

Example #2:

"Nurture a morning and evening routine that finds better ways to maximize my energy."

Here the goal is tweaked slightly to make it Progress based.

It's not reliant on a specific outcome; instead, it puts the emphasis on ideas and potential for progress. As long as you keep finding ways to improve it, you'll be succeeding with this goal.

If you keep improving, you're guaranteed to get results.

Setting Progress-Based Goals for Your Life Mission

Now that you understand how to set Progress based goals to keep improving and achieve what you want, it's your turn to set goals based on the Life Missions you realized in the last lesson.

But before learning about those steps, there's one thing you must know:

If you want to change everything in your life at once, it won't work.

A big reason why people can't stick with their goals is because they make too many or have too lofty ambitions. One of the biggest barriers that stands between you and your goals is becoming overwhelmed.

In our impatience for results, we try to change too much at once, and expect too much of ourselves; and this impatience usually leads to frustration and failure.

This is why most people fail to reach their goals.

To stick to your goal, you need a different strategy — *pick ONE Life Mission* to begin with.

Start with that, focus on it and take baby steps.

1. The One Thing You Want Most

Out of all the Life Missions you want to achieve, pick 1 to start with — *the one that you want MOST.* The aim here is to narrow down your focus.

When you're trying to make a lot of changes at once, it's hard and can demotivate you easily. This in turn will make you give up easily.

Don't worry that you're leaving all the rest of the Missions behind, you're just picking one to start with. If you can master this one at ease, you will be able to take on more Life Missions later!

So, choose one of the Life Missions you defined earlier that you want to create a Progress based goal for.

Write it down here:

2. Make It Specific

It is important to have a clear idea of what you want to achieve. That way you can focus your time and energy on achieving your goal and stay away from distractions.

Say you'd like to improve your relationships fulfillment and take it as your number one Life Mission now.

You may want to set a goal like this:

"Improve my relationship with my partner"

But this is a vague goal.

To make it more specific, you could say: *"Improve my relationship by increasing the time spent with my partner."*

So when you are specific on your goal, it's easier for you to identify all its components and work accordingly towards achieving it.

To make your goal specific, ask yourself these questions:

What exactly needs to be accomplished?

Who else will be involved?

Where will this take place?

3. Ensure It's Achievable

How realistic or actionable is your goal? Is it something you are able to achieve in your capacity?

Research into the facts and figures relevant to your goal. Then think about the resources available to you, such as your budget, skills and resources you have, and the help you can get, etc. Ask yourself if your goal makes sense in your situation.

A goal like this is not achievable:

"Improve my relationship by spending all my downtime with my partner."

We are only human and do need our own time to rest and take care of other things in life.

So, a more realistic and achievable goal could be:

"Improve my relationship by increasing the quality time spent with my partner."

To make your goal achievable, ask yourself these questions:

Do I have, or can I get, the resources needed to achieve the goal?

Is the goal reasonable for me? (neither out of reach nor too easy)

Am I willing to make these commitments to reach the goal?

Are the actions I plan to take likely to bring improvement?

Your Progress Based Goal

After going through the above questions, have you formed a solid goal to achieve your Life Mission?

Write down your final goal statement here:

Evaluating Success and Failure When Setting SMART Goals

Despite understanding what SMART goals are and how to effectively write them out, some of you will succeed in your goals while some of you will not.

That is the nature of goals. Despite your best efforts, sometimes you'll come out short. But that's okay because this reveals another aspect of goals.

You see, goals help us change in so many ways, and they themselves can change, too. As you work through your goals, you might make adjustments to them. Maybe you need a little more time, or you weren't expecting other life distractions to dig into your time. This is all part of maintaining a Progress mindset.

Regardless, here is how you want to approach and evaluate these aspects:

Evaluating Failure

Take failure as a learning opportunity. It's a chance for you to learn about yourself, your goal-setting strategy, and the goal itself. From there, you can take that information and begin to make adjustments before attempting the goal again.

It is essential that if you experience roadblocks or failure, you don't take them as a sign to give up. They are challenges and opportunities for growth and further adjustment. The key is to walk away from these aspects with more knowledge than before.

Evaluating Success

While this is a good opportunity to enjoy your rewards, you should also use this opportunity for reflection, perhaps even more than with failure.

Reaching a goal is great, but that often leads to the question of "What's next?" And for many people, this is not an easy question to answer. All in all, reaching success with a goal can lead to us stagnating, which is dangerous.

That's not to say we need to be constantly achieving and setting goals and forgetting what you've already accomplished.

You should certainly be celebrating ALL victories, big or small. Not only that, but it's key that we enjoy the results of our efforts.

However, there comes a point where we need to reflect on that success. What have you gained from that success? What can you do moving forward to achieve more?

What do you want to do next?

By asking deeper questions about what you have achieved, you can further develop yourself and narrow down what needs to be focused on next.

Wrapping Up

So far, we've examined the impact of a Progress mindset on your Life Missions. A Progress mindset can transform your goals into reality through a constant process of growth.

A Progress mindset is about looking at life as a flow instead of the results of fixed outcomes. With a Progress mindset, you will always have something to look forward to. The fact that you can be hopeful of a better tomorrow is a clue that you can grow.

Staying positive and hopeful can ensure you get through all of life's challenges.

As you achieve the mini-goals that help you make progress towards your bigger goals, reward yourself every single time.

By doing so, you will give yourself a boost of positive self-esteem and confidence which can cultivate motivation to accomplish the next task.

Remember, living a Full Life takes patience and practice, but it also opens up opportunities that you may have never imagined. Be sure to celebrate all your accomplishments, both big and small, and take note of all the progress you make along the way towards achieving a Full Life.

#04

CHAPTER

Self Control Systems

"Your net worth to the world is usually determined by what remains after your bad habits are subtracted from your good ones."
– Benjamin Franklin

So far we have looked at the importance of Life Aspects, Life Missions, your Life Purpose, and a Progress mindset. When you have all of these things working in your life — you'll have an unstoppable momentum that will carry you forward to success.

In this chapter, I'm going to be introducing you to the power of self-control systems, and how they tie everything together.

As I'll explain in detail shortly, self-control systems will allow you to maintain a Progress mindset — and let it work for you on autopilot.

So let's get started with a story about my own experience, where I once again found myself facing an obstacle.

"The Pain in My... Back"

In 2013, Lifehack was doing extremely well, and we were making great progress in all areas — including expanding our content offerings, and increasing our reader engagements and subscriber numbers.

However, change is inevitable—and that is when my health debt came calling!

For a long time, I'd suffered from severe back pain due to years of built-up stress, poor posture and general neglect for my physical health (clearly, I'd been failing to pay attention to all of my 6 Life Aspects).

I'd sacrificed my health for other areas in my life — and I was beginning to pay the price for this. I was learning the hard way that it's essential that we balance all 6 Life Aspects.

But things were about to get worse...

I woke up one morning and my back pain was so bad that I couldn't get out of bed without being in total agony! And this pain didn't subside. It was there when I tried sitting. And it was there when I tried walking. Worse still, when I went to bed that evening, the pain kept me awake all night.

I struggled for several days to try to overcome the pain, but nothing seemed to help. I couldn't exercise. I couldn't drive. And I couldn't find any relief from the excruciating pain.

To be honest, it was so crippling that within a few weeks it severely threatened my work and family life. That's because my whole focus was now on myself and the physical torture I was experiencing. I felt gradually powerless as my infirmity began to have effects on all areas of my life. My ability to manage Lifehack was hindered; and my social life was no more. And as I could no longer drive or walk, I was unable to take and get my kids from school.

Willpower was not enough to rescue me — the pain was just too severe.

I knew, though, that there was no one-off solution or quick-fix cure. I had to start changing multiple aspects of my life and factor in how each affected the other.

The immense pressure of this forced me to rethink everything I was doing. And I mean everything!

Eventually, however, this led me to a BIG realization...

All my life, I had been running on willpower — but I now understood that willpower was not enough, and instead, I needed a system that could automate many of the things that I did in my life. This was when I came up with the idea for self-control systems: a Progress mindset that runs on autopilot.

Initially, I tested the idea on my own life; but, once I saw its incredible power, I immediately began to roll it out at Lifehack. I also began to share the method with our readers. As I'll explain in a moment, the self-control systems I adopted transformed my daily routines — and subsequently, transformed my life.

In terms of my back problem, I started creating habits and routines that ensured I was no longer sacrificing my Physical Health Aspect. I also made sure that these new and improved habits were aligned with the other 5 Life Aspects.

Here are the steps I implemented.

Physical Health:

- Worked with a personal trainer to create an individualized program of back stretches and strengthening exercises.
- Changed my diet to cut out sugar and alcohol, and included more fresh fruits and veggies, and more nutrient dense meals (no more eating junk food on the run!).

Work:

- Invested in ergonomic chairs and standing desks for myself and everyone in our office.
- Encouraged regular meditation/contemplation breaks for all staff, including myself.

Spiritual Wellness:

- Incorporated deep relaxation and breathing exercises

into my daily routine (to help calm my mind and reduce the build-up of physical stress).

Mental Strength:

- Adopted a 'reading for gain' policy. This involved reading books on how to become fitter, healthier and stronger after injury.

Interestingly, as soon as I adopted these new habits and routines, I saw a massive boost in the two other Life Aspects.

Family & Relationships — These areas improved rapidly because I was soon able to move around again! I was in better shape and better spirits, which made it way more enjoyable to spend time with others (and for them to be around me!).

Money — As my energy returned, and my pain reduced, I was able to refocus on my work. I could travel to the office, attend meetings, and be a productive part of the Lifehack team again. I also noticed that as my pain decreased — my confidence increased. This helped me to think and work smarter.

These habits and routines formed the basis of the first self-control system that I created. And with this I was able to master my back pain and significantly strengthen my body.

But that's not all. Because I attacked the problem from a holistic perspective, I was able to boost all areas of my life.

For example, I'm much calmer and more focused than before due to the rest/breathing routines I created for myself. And in the office, I noticed that after introducing new habits and routines to my team, that it wasn't long before they were happier and more productive.

They genuinely appreciated the investment in the office. And they found the new routines just as powerful as I had.

To this day, my emphasis is always on having an efficient self-control system. After years of using these in my personal and professional life — I can confidently say they are tried-and-tested methods of success.

They worked for me; and they'll work for you.

Before I show you exactly how to create a self-control system, and how to put them into action in your life, let me just make one thing clear: Your habits and routines should never be set in stone. If they aren't working, then you should actively adapt them to suit your needs and end goals.

Self-control systems embed what you learn into patterns that form a regular part of your life (habits and routines) — and then reward you with consistent progress.

Interested to learn more? Then let's dive straight in.

How A Self-Control System Works

What's a self-control system?

The objective of a self-control system is basically to make your Progress mindset run on *autopilot*.

Life all comes down to your *daily* habits and routines.

Your habits control 80% of your daily actions and decisions. That means the vast majority of what you do is dictated by these habits. And you're not even aware of most of them because habits are basically programs you've set and follow subconsciously.

You can say that habits govern your life and where it's going. If you have weak and static habits; you'll struggle through life. If you have strong and progress based habits; you'll be a master of your life.

The self-control system makes use of habits and routines in an intelligent and efficient way — similar to "making your money work for you". Look at habits like *investments that return interest*. Good habits keep giving you regular rewards.

Essentially, when you have a good self-control system, you are practicing habits and routines that propel you to make progress towards your goals... almost effortlessly.

The Secret to "Sustainable"

Sustainable is what separates successful people from the rest of the world. And the key to keeping your progress sustainable is simple:

Manage your energy!

A lot of people only focus on how to manage their time and totally ignore energy. It's a lot like your car's fuel gauge. There's enough fuel to take you around, and there's some in reserve to carry you through tough times. So how do you ensure you'll always have enough fuel?

This is where a self-control system comes in. A self-control system will enable you to exert less of your mental and physical strength to make progress.

Think of it like riding a bicycle: at the beginning, you need to learn how to balance, to pedal, and steer simultaneously. You focus more on what's facing you than what's around you at this period. This is called the learning phase.

As soon as riding becomes a system—a point when you have mastered the tricks and internalized the skills— you can ride subconsciously. You'd realize you can multitask while riding the bike. You could raise your hands as you pedal, admire what's around you, converse with someone and even drink a bottle of water with one hand.

What if you can convert all the efforts you have been making into a sustainable system the exact same way? A system enables you to maintain your momentum on auto-pilot?

You can! And, next I'll explain how.

SELF CONTROL SYSTEMS
THE **3 KEY FACTORS** OF SUCCESS

1. PRACTICAL
2. ENERGY POSITIVE
3. PROGRESS BASED

Creating a Good System

It takes more than just having a set of goals to build a strong system. A good system maximizes your inner capacity to take on more challenging goals. A good system is *practical*. It offers concrete and real actions with an apparent intention.

For instance, a solid bedtime routine is concrete and possesses specific to-dos. It could include meditation, working out, and performing basic hygiene. It may also include organizing your outfit so you could save time the following morning. Those are clear and purposeful actions that affect your productivity the next day

The second factor that makes a good system is what is known as *energy positive.*

A system that is energy positive provides you with a net gain in mental and physical energy. From our example of maintaining an evening routine, every effort you make each evening provides you with a huge gain in terms of better mental health, healthy sleep habits, and will provide you with time savings for the following morning. This will build up overtime and offer you unlimited momentum for better productivity throughout your day.

The third success factor that makes a good self-control system is to make sure it's *progress-based.* Yup, progress is a major factor once again.

A good system should include aspects that you can track and assess to improve it as needed, to revisit anything that isn't working, and to continually set you on track with your Life Missions and towards your North Star.

Self-control systems are constantly evolving and should be thought of as a foundation that you can build on and mould as needed. As you continue to grow, so will your self-control system. So, in short, a self-control system is simply a way to harness everything together, and in turn, it will begin to produce powerful momentum on its own. Let's take a look at an example that you may relate to, and see how powerful a self-control system can really be.

Don's Story

Don came to me wanting to make a positive change his life, but he was unsure where to start. He was working at a desk job fulltime and not making enough money. His relationships with his wife and kids were tense and often filled with arguments. He was neglecting his self care and was feeling the effects worsen every day.

He no longer felt excited about life and because of his poor physical and mental health, he was starting to slip on his job. This created further problems as he feared losing his job.

I'm sure you can see where this goes... Don was miserable.

So, I introduced him to the idea of shifting his mindset to a Full Life Mindset. He needed to first see that he held a wonderful opportunity to make some big changes in his life. And, that everything was connected.

As I worked with Don and broke down how he managed his time, I noticed that he spent almost 3 hours after work sitting in front of the television eating junk food and drinking soda!

This habit alone was absolutely impacting his physical health, his relationships with his family, his self esteem, and ultimately his performance at his job. I told him that changing just this one *daily habit* could completely revitalize multiple parts of his life at the same time. He didn't believe me at first, but I persisted. This is what we did.

We set a goal to spend at least 60 minutes every day exercising (in any capacity) where he would normally watch television. This would not only get him moving where he'd ordinarily be sedentary, Don also wouldn't be consuming mindless amounts of empty calories while doing so. He could do anything: walk around the neighborhood, dance, go on a hike, run on a treadmill, lift weights, do an aerobic video... it didn't matter, as long as he was exercising, he was making progress.

This was the start of Don's self-control system. By building a system that started with good progress based habits, he was setting himself up for success. The magic of a self-control system is that it keeps going, even without you exerting any extra effort—and it gets bigger and better!

So, Don started with a habit of exercising 60 minutes a day. Simple enough. But guess what happened? His self-control system kicked into overdrive.

To start his new regimen, Don took advantage of this opportunity to make his workout "fun".

He purchased a Sony Playstation (which he figured would benefit the whole family) and also bought the game "Just Dance"—a group dance game where you follow prompts on the screen to dance with up to 6 other people.

He decided that where he would usually plop down with the television remote, he would instead start a game of "Just Dance." Immediately, Don's family got on board with his new routine.

They loved this new activity so much that they went from spending 60 minutes a day bonding over this new game to spending no less than 90 minutes a day together!

Yet, the benefits reached even beyond his family.

As Don started exercising, he found himself with a clearer and more positive mindset—he could feel the stress melt away from work once he began dancing.

His family was certainly enjoying it, too! The quality time they were now having with each other was unlike anything they'd experienced before.

And, as he began to shed excess weight and build muscle from all the dancing, he felt more confident because his clothes were fitting better and he could sustain physical activity for much longer.

He started to gain a mental clarity that he never had before. He would come home and have energy to spend quality time with his family and the mental ability to make additional plans that the family would enjoy.

Because he was now exercising, he was sleeping better. This affected his performance at work, as well as his demeanor at home.

He is now more optimistic about his career, and is considering how he can grow on the job.

He now sees his obstacle of being unhappy at work as an opportunity to make a positive change towards what he wants.

And, one unexpected consequence of Don's new routine?

He and his wife found that they love dancing so much, that they actually joined a dance class together, which has vastly improved their relationship. As you can see, just taking positive and progress based action in one area of your life—in one Life Aspect—can affect many areas.

Don was able to make a pretty major impact to his life by making a commitment to working out just 60 minutes a day. He now sees the value of a self-control system and the potential for radical change in his life.

The most impressive thing about Don's story? His shift in mindset—a new understanding of the power of progress and its amazing ability to create momentum—is what got him where he is now, and it is what will continue to propel him forward as he creates new goals and milestones in his life.

All it took was for him to shift his thinking, and he was well on his way to living a Full Life.

Your Self-Control System Assessment

Take the following quick assessment to find out how strong your self-control system is across the 6 Life Aspects: Physical Health, Family & Relationships Fulfillment, Work & Career Prosperity, Money & Wealth Satisfaction, Spiritual Wellness, Mental Strength.

Simply read each statement carefully and circle one of the five options for each statement indicating how well that statement describes you:

1. Statement does not describe you at all
2. Statement describes you very little
3. Statement describes you somewhat
4. Statement describes you pretty well
5. Statement describes you exactly

Remember to circle your best, most honest answer.

Physical Health

1. I am aware that I have some bad habits that affect my health.

2. I have a healthy eating plan and stick to it.

3. I have an exercise routine and workout regularly.

4. I have successfully built a good habit or quit a bad habit related to my health over the past 5 years.

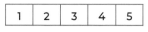

5. I have a morning routine to help me stay energetic.

6. I have a bedtime routine to help me sleep better.

7. I reward myself when I accomplish a health goal / milestone.

Family & Relationships Fulfillment

1. I am aware that I have some bad habits that affect my relationships with my partner, kids, or family.

1	2	3	4	5

2. I have a plan to improve my relationships and stick to it.

1	2	3	4	5

3. I schedule time to nurture my relationships.

1	2	3	4	5

4. I have successfully built a good habit or quit a bad habit related to my relationships over the past 5 years.

1	2	3	4	5

5. I have a daily routine that consists of time for my relationships.

1	2	3	4	5

6. I have a habit of having meaningful conversations with the ones I love and care for regularly.

1	2	3	4	5

7. I reward myself when my loved ones feel happy because of what I've done.

1	2	3	4	5

Work & Career Prosperity

1. I am aware that I have some bad habits that affect my work performance.

2. I have a career plan and stick to it.

3. I have a routine that helps me work productively.

4. I have successfully built a good habit or quit a bad habit related to my work and career over the past 5 years.

5. I have a morning routine to help me stay energetic.

6. I have no difficulty staying focused.
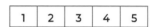

7. I reward myself when I accomplish a goal / milestone at work.
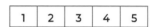

Money & Wealth Satisfaction

		1	2	3	4	5
1.	I am aware that I have some bad habits that affect my financial situation.	1	2	3	4	5
2.	I have a financial / budget plan and stick to it.	1	2	3	4	5
3.	I have a routine that helps me save money.	1	2	3	4	5
4.	I have successfully built a good habit or quit a bad habit related to money and wealth over the past 5 years.	1	2	3	4	5
5.	I have a way to prevent overspending.	1	2	3	4	5
6.	I have good credit score.	1	2	3	4	5
7.	I reward myself when I accomplish a money goal / milestone.	1	2	3	4	5

Spiritual Wellness

1. I am aware that I have some bad habits that affect my mood and emotions.

1	2	3	4	5

2. I have a plan to better regulate my emotions and stick to it.

1	2	3	4	5

3. I have a routine that consists of time for self-care.

1	2	3	4	5

4. I have successfully built a good habit or quit a bad habit related to spiritual wellness over the past 5 years.

1	2	3	4	5

5. I have a way to calm my thoughts and feelings.

1	2	3	4	5

6. I have sufficient "me" time.

1	2	3	4	5

7. I reward myself when I overcome my negative thoughts.

1	2	3	4	5

Mental Strength

1. I am aware that I have some bad habits that affect my self-confidence.

| 1 | 2 | 3 | 4 | 5 |

2. I have a plan to grow my mental strength and stick to it.

| 1 | 2 | 3 | 4 | 5 |

3. I have a routine that consists of time for self-improvement and personal growth.

| 1 | 2 | 3 | 4 | 5 |

4. I have successfully built a good habit or quit a bad habit related to mental strength over the past 5 years.

| 1 | 2 | 3 | 4 | 5 |

5. I have a way to not let myself give up easily.

| 1 | 2 | 3 | 4 | 5 |

6. I have very resilience when the going gets tough.

| 1 | 2 | 3 | 4 | 5 |

7. I reward myself when I overcome a tough challenge.

| 1 | 2 | 3 | 4 | 5 |

Now, it's time to find out what the scores mean!

First, calculate the score you get for each Life Aspect:

	Score
Physical Health	
Family & Relationships Fulfillment	
Work & Career Prosperity	
Money & Wealth Satisfaction	
Spiritual Wellness	
Mental Strength	

The higher you score for a Life Aspect (out of 35), the higher the level of self-control you have for that Life Aspect.

Next, calculate the overall self-control you have.

Level of Overall Self Control = Total Score for All Life Aspects / 210 x 100%

For example:

If your Total Score for All Life Aspects (adding up all the scores for the Life Aspects) is 95, the overall self-control you have is:

95/210 x 100% = 45%

Which means, you're reaching 45% potential of your self-control system.

What's your overall self-control currently?

Calculate it and write it down:

Understanding the importance of a self-control system, and how you're doing with your current system gives you a better idea of where you are at now.

Maybe you have a relatively strong self-control system in Work & Career Prosperity but a weak one in Physical Health, or maybe overall speaking you don't have a very concrete self-control system; whatever the case is, you have the power to strengthen the system and achieve the goals you want.

Wrapping Up

I hope from this chapter you can see how incredibly impactful having a self-control system can be. Once you get one started, you can continuously build upon it to improve your life every single day.

In the next chapter, I'm going to finally dive into the concept of Life Multipliers. After building a solid foundation so far, these are the skills that will push your scale of change above and beyond what you thought a single person could do before.

"It is never too late to be what you might have been."

– George Eliot

#05

CHAPTER

The Power of Life Multipliers

"Twenty years from now you will be more disappointed by the things you didn't do than by the things you did."

– *Mark Twain*

We've covered a lot of ground so far, and in this chapter I'm going to explain a few key concepts that tie everything together and will help you live a Full Life.

And, I'm going to start with an insightful piece of knowledge that I hope will energize you.

You can actually become more productive in every area of your life by doing less. And, not only can you achieve more, but you will find yourself having increased spare time to spend with family and friends — not to mention a chance to enjoy the hobbies you love but have neglected.

This is the Full Life Framework in action.

In this chapter, we'll talk about Life Multipliers, and how they can not only help you gain work life harmony but help you to take it all to the next level.

Life Multipliers

The final piece of the success puzzle lies in Life Multipliers. What exactly are Life Multipliers? Well, simply put, they are things that are what allow you to *multiply your ability, influence and effectiveness.*

These are the true keys to unlocking your full potential and increasing your personal scale beyond limits. The cool thing about Life Multipliers is that they are something that most, if not all, of us are familiar with, but often go unthought of as something that can be improved upon. But the truth is, they are skills just like anything else, and the more you hone them, the more they work for you.

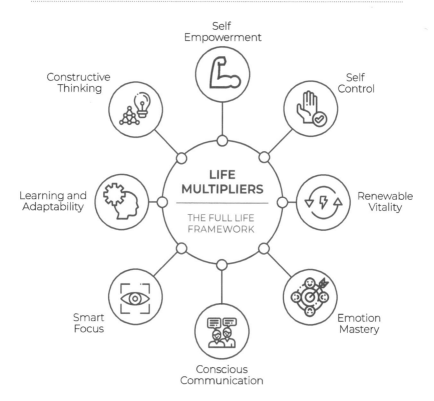

Recall the comparison I made in Chapter 2 about having a hard time putting a piece of furniture from IKEA together without all the parts. These parts act just as the 6 Life Aspects. And, the tools that you'll need to build the furniture are how you can think of Life Multipliers.

How I discovered Life Multipliers was due to my fascination with continuous improvement. It all started with me wanting to turn something as intangible as "personal drive" into a skill that could be systematically taught and improved.

Frankly, I was sick of relying on circumstances to create my motivation. And, it seemed that I had tried everything—reading daily quotes, journaling, setting reminder goals in my calendar. But each of these tactics were too one-off, and disconnected.

I wanted something solid that I could rely on consistently when I needed a boost of motivation, or even a longer stretch to get a big project done; something that would enable me to spark motivation at any time and any place.

So, I decided that logic was the solution here. I simply applied all the previous principles from the Full Life mindset and turned motivation into a skill. This was the first Life Multiplier—and from there I realized that mastering something like motivation as a skill can completely transform your life in every aspect. So, why couldn't it be done with more?

The result became the 8 Life Multipliers we teach at Lifehack today. These Life Multipliers impact your ability to positively influence the world around you—how far it reaches, and how much change you can create in your own and others' lives. We all want this in our lives, but we can only do so much. And, there's certainly a limit on the amount of time and energy we each have.

But, that's the beauty of Life Multipliers. With them, you'll be able to dramatically increase your potential, and they'll actually begin working in your favor the more you hone them.

Life Multipliers increase your scale. Even with progress based goals and self-control systems—there are hundreds of areas in your life that need them. So where to start? Where to focus?

Focus on Life Multipliers, the skills that form a core and are relevant to many parts of your life. Invest, and keep investing in them. It's the only way to achieve massive success within a lifetime.

Recall the importance of time—and how it is such a precious and limited resource. Life Multipliers will enable you to greatly increase your effectiveness across many things at once. Therefore, these are the most valuable areas you can invest your time and energy in.

Let's go through the Life Multipliers one by one.

Self Empowerment:

Think of Self-Empowerment like the engine that runs a car. The stronger the engine, the more powerful your car is. Without this skill you're constantly running out of gas — or find it really hard to push when you're going uphill. A person with strong Self-Empowerment is crystal clear about their purpose, and has the ability to motivate themselves on demand, with concrete plans of action.

Self-Empowerment means taking charge of your own life by way of the decisions you make every single day—it's about taking responsibility for your actions. By setting goals that harness your abilities and strengths, and maintaining a Progress mindset, you will be more empowered. Create a Full Life by focusing on fostering habits and routines that lead to growth and increase your happiness.

Self-Control/Habits:

Think of Self-Control as the complementary skill to Self-Empowerment. So if Self-Empowerment is the engine, Self-Control is the steering wheel. It gives you the discipline and strength to stay on track with your direction.

A person with Self-Control knows how to set clear goals and consistently follows through with them. They know how to build constructive habits and routines that support their goals, and design them in a way that makes sure that they stick.

One of our amazing writers, Amanda Light, shares this on Self-Control: *Instead of acting on immediate impulses, self-control can help us to control our emotions and help prevent us from doing anything we'll regret, like enjoying that delicious chocolate milkshake when you've been trying to eat healthier.*

Exercising Self-Control in these types of situations eventually leads to success and big achievement.

Not only is Self-Control important in achieving personal goals and underlies any successful person, it is also extremely important in our social lives. Using Self-Control is part of our everyday interactions with others. More often than not, we are put in situations that cause stress or friction within us that may be caused by other people, and the power to control your feelings and emotions in these situations will make or break you.

Giving into impulsive emotions and feelings can have bad consequences, and knowing how to use self-control will save you from some pretty awkward situations.

Renewable Vitality/Motivation:

Remember how energy is one of the two key resources you've got to manage? Well this is the skill behind keeping your energy levels high — and making sure that you can replenish it fast enough.

A person with Renewable Vitality maintains a high energetic baseline. To achieve it, they're physically fit and healthy because they eat right, exercise regularly, and have healthy lifestyle habits.

So, take care of your body! Watch what you eat and aim for nutritionally dense foods over processed junk foods. Drink at least eight 8 ounces glasses of water every day. Aim to exercise at least 30 minutes each day. Practice self care. Treat yourself with kindness and love so you can be the very best version of you.

If you practice these efforts and turn them into habits, you'll notice your energy will skyrocket, and that will affect every area of your life in a positive way.

Emotion Mastery:

Emotion Mastery is how you manage your mindsets. Because mindsets are your thinking patterns, they subconsciously dictate how you think and feel about something.

Your mindsets dictate whether something makes you feel positive or negative, and the decisions that result from those feelings.

And a person with a highly developed Emotion Mastery skill is able to consciously manage their subconscious by being aware of their thinking patterns to reframe a situation and change the way they feel about it into something positive. Adopting a Progress mindset, using Positive Affirmations, Setting SMART goals, and aiming for a Full Life mindset are the first steps to Emotion Mastery.

Conscious Communication:

Conscious Communication focuses on how to make meaningful connections with people.

A person with Conscious Communication listens and expresses with purpose. They can understand other people's ideas while being able to deliver their own thoughts and feelings clearly.

Mat Apocada, one of Lifehack's top writers, says it best:

Effective communication is about how all of us interact and communicate in every aspect of our lives. It's the ability to say something at the right time; to be able to get multiple people on the same page in a group decision. It's how that one friend of yours who plans most of the activities is able to get everyone to the same place at the same time.

Non-verbal communication is key to being effective as well. It's the ability to have your body language say the right thing so the person you're speaking to knows you're listening.

Effective communicators don't react to situations with high emotion. It means not having to say something all the time in every situation. You are even being an effective communicator when you show up to pick your daughter up from the mall when you say you will. You are communicating to her that she can rely on you.

Smart Focus:

Smart Focus is the skill behind managing your energy and time in harmony.

Most people sacrifice one for the other — they might rush to get something done and drain themselves of energy. Or they might do something really comfortably but waste a lot of time doing it. Smart Focus is the art of getting the best of both worlds — being effective in both time and energy at the same time.

A master of Smart Focus is able to increasingly do a lot more by doing less overall.

Identify what's distracting you and compartmentalize tasks like responding to email only at specific times in your day. If you're a chronic multi-tasker, it's time to hang up that hat and focus on one thing at a time.

Above all, develop productive habits that lead to efficient routines so that deep focus becomes the norm for you. You have all the tools you need to figure out how to focus on the things that matter most to you. It's time to give your work your undivided attention.

Learning and Adaptability:

This is the essential skill that helps you to stay relevant and keep your mind sharp. Nowadays, our modern society moves at a breakneck pace. Change happens in the blink of an eye!

We can't rely on slow and traditional methods of learning to keep up anymore.

So a person with Learning and Adaptability can master any knowledge and skill fast. They have the right mindsets and the toolkit to respond to change swiftly and make sure they never stop making progress.

Pam Thomas, another one of our top writers at Lifehack summarizes it well.

When we learn, we expand our knowledge base obviously but it goes much further than that. Learning can help us to step out of a pattern or routine. The more we do that, the more confidence we create.

It moves us past that point of complacency. It in turn enhances and improves the skills we already have by helping us to not only strengthen them, but also add to them.

It is also beneficial to our health. While it may not cure diseases like Alzheimer's, for example, it has been reported that learning can slow the progression of diseases that impact the brain.

Constructive/Creative Thinking:

This is the skill that determines how efficiently you can think. The most successful people are able to process information and make the right decisions with speed and confidence.

A person with Constructive Thinking has a clear mind and organized thinking patterns. They can easily make connections between different ideas and look at things from different angles — which makes them amazing problem solvers.

On the surface, these are people who seem to be naturally smart. In fact, it's a core skill that you can train yourself to have too.

Creativity at its heart, is being able to see things in a way that others cannot. It's a skill that helps you find new perspectives to create new possibilities and solutions to different problems.

Everything, including brilliant inventions, cannot come from nothing; it all derives from some sort of inspiration. Creativity works by connecting things together in order to derive new meaning or value. When you use your creative ability and constructive thinking to turn your limitations and setbacks into opportunities, you'll find doors opening for you in areas you may have never imagined.

Remember, your attitude is also important when it comes to achieving a goal, and tackling a setback or problem. That's because a positive attitude transforms not just your mental state, but your physical and emotional well being. It is the key to lasting total transformation.

How the Multipliers Contribute to the 6 Life Aspects

Here's a visual guide to show you how each skill contributes to different aspects of life:

Skills	Physical Health	Family & Relationships Fulfillment	Work & Career Prosperity	Wealth & Money Satisfaction	Spiritual Wellness	Mental Strength
Self-Empowerment	✔	✔	✔	✔	✔	✔
Self-Control	✔	✔	✔	✔	✔	✔
Renewable Vitality	✔	✔	✔	✔	✔	✔
Emotion Mastery		✔	✔		✔	✔
Conscious Communication		✔	✔			
Smart Focus	✔		✔	✔		
Learning & Adaptability			✔			
Constructive Thinking			✔			

Give Yourself a Visual Pep Talk

The objects of our focus can determine our perception of reality. Visualization is an excellent tool that can be used to shape our own reality and it actually has a biological explanation behind it.

It's called the reticular activating system. The (RAS) is a network of neurons in the brain that determines what sensory information we perceive from our environment and what will remain unnoticed. It prioritizes everything that concerns our survival and safety as well as the things that match the current content of our minds: beliefs, thoughts, emotions, etc.

Basically, your RAS constantly looks for data in your environment that matches and reinforces your thoughts and belief systems. Think of your RAS like your inner GPS. If you want your GPS to work to your advantage — you must program it accordingly.

And the best way to program it is by visualizing your goals.

If you visualize yourself accomplishing something you believe you can't do — and do it several times (repetition is important!) — you'll begin to override the old, limiting beliefs that prevented you from succeeding with a new belief: your capacity to achieve it.

So, now that you have the Full Life Framework at your fingertips, it's really important that you recognize your own power in your life. Notice your strengths, your accomplishments, and your ability to overcome challenges in the past

I want you to reflect so far on everything you've learned. What does your very best future look like? Where will you be? Truly visualize this and sit with it for several minutes. See it as a reality.

Now, think about all the things you've accomplished and the small victories you've achieved. Revisit Chapter 3 and read over the Positive Affirmations. Pat yourself on the back for making it this far.

Recapping The Essentials

Living a Full Life means being able to experience the richness and meaning across the entire spectrum of life. But, remember, it doesn't mean having a "perfect" life, because there's no such thing as a perfect life.

No matter how rich, powerful, or how lucky you are, there will always be challenges, obstacles, and failure. Living a Full Life means embracing these challenges, and having the determination to drive positive change in all of them.

So, there are 6 fundamental parts of life that you must fulfill in order to feel whole: Physical Health, Family & Relationships, Wealth and Money Satisfaction, Work & Career Prosperity, Spiritual Wellness, and Mental Strength. We call these the 6 Life Aspects.

Together, these 6 Life Aspects provide you with all the rich and meaningful experiences you can have in life. These are the MUST-HAVES in your life. Without them, you'll feel like something is missing and have a sense of emptiness or loss. Yet, having success in these aspects gives you a feeling of confidence, hope and a true sense of security.

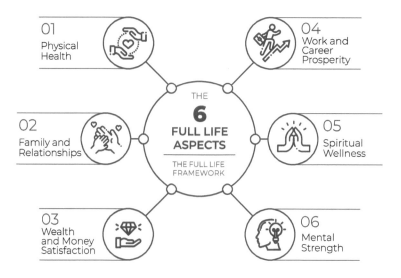

Life Missions

The 6 Full Life Aspects are categories to help you to evaluate your life, but everyone has different needs and different circumstances. That's where Life Missions come into play. Your life is unique, so to make these 6 Life Aspects meaningful to you — you have to apply them on your own terms.

Recall that a Life Mission is simply a mission in your own life that provides you with satisfaction and meaning and is intrinsically motivating—meaning, coming from within yourself, not from external motivators.

These are what makes your life worth living.

Each of your Life Missions should fulfill a big fundamental inner desire in your life.

You're guaranteed to have at least one Inner Desire, or Life Mission, for each of the 6 Life Aspects.

Life Missions are super important to your sense of fulfillment because they:

1. Give meaning to your key life aspects.
2. Help you fulfill your major inner desires.

In short, Life Missions help you define what you're actually looking for in life. When you make it a mission it means you are making a commitment to yourself and will not compromise — because you know that they are the most valuable things in your life.

And, when you commit to a mission, you'll be motivated to find a way to accomplish it no matter what.

Progress Mindset

So how can we make sure we're always staying true to our Life Missions no matter what obstacles or challenges get the way? It comes down to the right mindset. There are two types of mindsets: a Static mindset and a Progress mindset.

The main characteristic of a Static mindset is that it focuses on the outcome. It defaults to seeing things purely in terms of success or failure. If you don't achieve the outcome you expect then you haven't succeeded... which means you have failed.

This can prompt you to question and doubt your ability, your willpower, and your fulfillment in life. It gives you a certain default thinking pattern through a negative filter, and then you make decisions based on this negative baseline.

On the other hand, there is a Progress mindset. Instead of focusing on outcomes, or outputs, a Progress mindset focuses on the efforts you invest into what you're trying to achieve—in other words, the progress you are making. As you can never be 100% in control of the outcome (which is what a Static mindset is based upon), you can control your improvement — and you can measure it, plan it, and practice it. This is why a Progress mindset is so valuable. There will always be progress to be made—actions to follow up with and things to improve, which means there's always something to look forward to.

Being "positive" isn't about just being "happy" and always "looking at the bright side" of things. Real positivity is having a Progress mindset, as this type of thinking guarantees you will always be better off regardless of whether an outcome is within your expectations or not.

Self-Control Systems

It's also important to be putting in consistent actions that are sustainable. If everyone was able to make their inputs sustainable everyone would always reach their goals.

It's not just a matter of willpower. Our mental and physical energy is limited—no matter how strong you start out, problems, obstacles and distractions will always appear on the way.

When your energy is at a low point, that's when those blockers start to take a hold over you. And, if you try to push too far, you'll likely end up burning out. For it to be sustainable— you have to manage your energy.

This is where self-control systems come into the picture. A self-control system usually takes the form of habits and routines that help you do things without a lot of mental or physical effort.

If you can convert all of the actions into systems, then you can then focus your willpower on things that get you closer to new goals instead of spending it all just trying to maintain the status quo.

A good system transcends any single goal. In fact, a good system is like a tower that keeps getting taller as you build on top of the foundation. It helps you increase your raw personal capability to pursue ever higher, more challenging goals.

Another factor of a good control system is what we call energy positive. Energy positive means it reduces your burden in the long run and gives you a net gain in mental and/or physical energy.

The third factor of success is that it's progress based. You don't just want a series of static habits and routines that never change. A good system has aspects that you can measure and evaluate to constantly improve it. So, to make progress sustainable you can't rely on pure willpower alone.

Great self-control systems help you move forward on auto-pilot to let you focus your energy on places where you want to make breakthroughs.

Another factor is time.

Everyone has a set amount of time in life. No more, no less. Between the busy demands of family, work, and everyday life, we really don't have that much time to spend freely at all. And we've only got a limited time to fulfill our Life Missions. So if we want big positive change — we have to shorten the amount of time it takes to make a lot of progress.

Life Multipliers

These are skills that can give you 5x or even 10x your progress in one or more life aspects at the same time. These are probably the most valuable areas you can invest your time and energy into, because the more Life Multipliers you discover and apply, the more freedom and power you'll have to push your Life Missions further.

And Life Multipliers are centered around what we call the "Key 20%": this natural phenomenon where generally 20 percent of your activities will account for 80 percent of your results. If you focus on skills that form the Key 20% — and you keep developing them further and further, the other 80% of results they account for will just keep getting bigger and better.

The beauty of these skills is that they're skills that will always be relevant no matter what stage of life you're in, or what circumstances you're facing.

They're also skills that will only keep giving you better and better results. If you're going to invest time and energy into anything, investing in these 8 skills is the most guaranteed investment you can ever make for yourself.

Cultivating the Most Needed Skills

Developing all these 8 skills at once could be overwhelming. So instead of trying to improve them all, prioritize the skills you need to learn based on the Life Aspects you suffer most.

Let's identify the Life Aspects that score lowest in the self-assessment.

Which Life Aspects do you score lowest in?
Choose no more than 3 of them:

Now, do you see any skills that directly contribute to more than one of your selected Life Aspects? Which are the most relevant skills for you? List them down:

So these are the skills that you should prioritize developing now because they are the Multipliers that can get you closer to living a Full Life sooner!

Strive for Work-Life Harmony

One more tip before I go...

We often hear about work life balance: having a good balance between work and personal time. Whilst this may sound like a smart idea, it can also imply that we should dedicate at least half of our time to work–and sacrifice time for our "personal life".

The truth is, it's nearly impossible to split your time equally between the two. And, you may end up stressing out if you're not able to meet that expectation of balance.

Instead, why not think of having work life harmony instead?

With this mindset, you can actually integrate work into your life in a way that feels more complete. This way, you don't need to view work and having personal time as separate. So, how do you achieve work life harmony?

The difference between work life balance and work life harmony is pretty simple. With the former, there is an implication that you have to sacrifice your "life" for work. But, this is the worst way to go about things!

How can you truly be at peace in life if you dread 8 hours of your day?

Work life harmony on the other hand, allows your work to be a part of your life. This means that you can choose to be happy both at home, and at work! Work no longer needs to be seen as the 'bad' or un-fun activity.

Having work life harmony also ensures you're truly present in whatever place you find yourself. Just take a look at Jeff Bezos, CEO of Amazon for example. He uses a non traditional approach to work by making time for breakfast every morning with his family, doesn't set his alarm before going to bed, schedules surprisingly few meetings, and still puts aside a few minutes every day to wash his own dishes.

He believes that all his staff should stop trying to achieve a 'balance' in their work and personal lives as that implies a trade off. Instead, he envisions a more holistic relationship between the two.

Creating work life harmony is also about understanding yourself–which includes your limitations and past obstacles–as this allows you to become more resilient.

If you never had to experience struggles, challenges or setbacks, then you would never be forced to adapt and mature. So in theory, having to face obstacles in life is actually quite necessary.

Most of us think of setbacks and obstacles as negative. Though, if you're able to maintain an optimistic attitude, you'll almost always have a higher chance of success of overcoming those obstacles to reach your eventual goal.

Your attitude towards setbacks will define the outcome of whether you rise from the challenge or remain stuck in it. So, in order to achieve work life harmony, it's important to have a resilient attitude as challenges will always come your way–

especially when you strive to integrate work into your life, and not a separate or dominant part of life.

Living in harmony is about feeling good about the ways in which you spend your time, despite how busy you may be. Your switch from work mode to a more personal mode should be effortless. It's about integrating your personal life and the things you love into your busy work life!

It all begins with a shift in perspective. Understanding what your passions are, and learning to be resilient, before taking a different approach to the way you manage your time and everyday tasks.

These are steps that you can start taking to move away from balance to harmony.

Take the Next Step

As you have hopefully gathered by now, at Lifehack, we're all about progress. So, I encourage you to continue on your progressive journey after you finish this book, and to let Lifehack guide you.

First, here's what Lifehack is not about: learning knowledge for the sake of knowledge, presenting abstract theories that you can't apply to the real world, and sharing random feel good slogans and images.

While we do share powerful mindsets, inspirational stories and ideas, they're all for a purpose. That purpose is to help you make things happen. We want to turn your dreams and ideas into actionable steps. So we teach simple, practical insights and knowledge that you can apply in your daily life — to make immediate positive change, take ownership and gain control of your life to Live Fully.

Creating lasting happiness isn't easy. Happiness takes hard work! That means you've got to be in the driver's seat. It's up to you to master self control and self discipline. We can teach you what, why and how, but at the end of the day, you are the one that makes it happen.

If you can achieve it, you'll gain a whole new feeling of energy and zest for life that will change not only you, but the people around you. Something like that is more valuable than any amount of money in the world.

We offer several ways to do this:

Lifehack Insider Newsletter

We have a wonderful community of individuals we like to call "Lifehack Insiders". In this community I send out a special daily email newsletter to over 500,000 subscribers. Here I share tips, insights, educational advice and special promotions to all Insiders. Be sure to subscribe if you haven't yet done so! I'd love to hear from you!

The Lifehack Show

The Lifehack Show is a bi-weekly podcast that features experts from all over the world who share insights and advice about

Lifehack core issues. We cover all the hottest trends and takes on how to live your best life without sacrifice. Find new episodes by going to Lifehack's Podcast page on our website.

Lifehack Academy

At Lifehack Academy, we offer several online courses that will help you not only maintain a Full Life mindset, but take your life to the next level.

Actionable Motivation on Demand

When you're in a motivated state of mind, you're at your peak state of performance. There is a lot of material out there about motivation and getting into an energetic state of mind. The truth is, motivation needs to be on demand because you can't really rely on circumstances to make you feel motivated all the time. You need to be able to generate motivation when you need it.

This course teaches you to have boundless motivational energy that converts to meaningful action on demand right when you need it.

Learn Anything Fast

Let go of the past burdens and struggles you associated with learning and free yourself from traditional models that were never right for you.

In this course, you'll start from a fresh slate and rediscover your unique passion and methods for learning.

This course is about how to learn effectively with practical application in mind.

It's not about memorizing facts or knowledge for the sake of "knowing things".

Learning with intention means to make deliberate positive change in your life. Here, you'll learn to empower yourself to learn anything you want and be able to apply it immediately.

Laser Focus with Purpose

Do you feel constantly overwhelmed with your to-do list? Too busy to get anything done? We created this course just for you.

This course will teach you how to free yourself from this busy trap. Using Lifehack's tried and true methods to achieve more while doing less, you'll establish a new dynamic balance, and regain the time and energy to invest in meaningful things once more.

Are You Ready to Take Your Life to the Next Level?

Congrats! You've successfully made it through all the concepts behind our Full Life Framework! Once you start implementing this advice into your life, you'll notice major changes, starting immediately.

By now I hope you're happily adopting a Progress mindset. Remember, if you've had a change of mindset after reading this book, you've already accomplished a major victory... so celebrate!

The next step is to check out all that Lifehack has to offer. And, don't forget to take The Full Life Assessment if you haven't yet done so and start putting The Full Life Framework into action!

https://www.lifehack.org/life-assessment-quiz

"*The victory of success is half won when one gains the habit of setting goals and achieving them.*"

— *Og Mandino*

Recommended Reading

Atomic Habits by *James Clear*

Blink: The Power of Thinking Without Thinking
by Malcolm Gladwell

How Not to Die: Discover the Foods Scientifically Proven to
Prevent and Reverse Disease *by Michael Greger M.D. FACLM*

How We Learn: The Surprising Truth About When, Where,
and Why It Happens by Benedict Carey Man's Search for
Meaning *by Victor E. Frankl*

Make It Stick: The Science of Successful Learning
by Peter C. Brown

Make Your Bed: Little Things That Can Change Your Life...
And Maybe the World *by William H. McRaven*

Smarter, Faster, Better: The Secrets of Being Productive in Life
and Business *by Charles Duhigg*

The Emotion Code: How to Release Your Trapped Emotions
for Abundant Health, Love, and Happiness
by Dr. Bradley Nelson

The Four Agreements *by Don Miguel Ruiz*

The Happiness Advantage: How a Positive Brain Fuels Success in Work and Life *by Shawn Achor*

The Men's Health Big Book of Exercises: Four Weeks to a Leaner, Stronger, More Muscular You! *by Adam Campbell*

The Power of Habit: Why We Do What We Do in Life and Business *by Charles Duhigg*

The Power of Now: A Guide to Spiritual Enlightenment *by Eckhart Tolle*

The Women's Health Big Book of Exercises: Four Weeks to a Leaner, Sexier, Healthier You! *by Adam Campbell*

Why We Sleep: Unlocking the Power of Sleep and Dreams *by Matthew Walker PhD*

Words That Work: It's Not What You Say, It's What People Hear *by Frank Luntz*

You Are a Badass: How to Stop Doubting Your Greatness and Start Living an Awesome Life *by Jen Sincero*

About Leon Ho

Leon Ho is the Founder and CEO of Lifehack, which he started in 2005 as a way to share his personal productivity hacks to make life easier. Since then, he has grown Lifehack into one of the most read productivity, health and lifestyle websites in the world - with over 12 million monthly readers.

With over 12 years' experience, Leon is still just as passionate about pushing his limits and sharing his secrets about personal development as he was when he began. Through Leon's efforts, today Lifehack is a world class team that still retains its start up mentality where he has personally coached over 70 executives to make personal breakthroughs at work and at home. He is a valued guest speaker and contributor and has been featured in multiple publications, including at the UC Berkeley Hass School of Business, Harvard College in Asia Program, the Guardian, and the Washington Post, and was recognized as Business Week's #4 "Top 24 Young Asian Entrepreneurs".

Leon spends his spare time coaching his 2 sons, preparing them to be the next generation of productivity gurus.